STAR WARS INSIDER PRESENTS

THE MANDALORIAN COLLECTION

WELCOME...

There is a passage in Donald F. Glut's original novelization of *The Empire Strikes Back* that introduces the bounty hunter, Boba Fett. Glut wrote, "A human bounty hunter, Boba Fett was known for his extremely ruthless methods. He was dressed in a weapons covered, armored spacesuit, the kind worn by a group of evil warriors defeated by the Jedi Knights during the Clone Wars."

This, combined with Joe Johnston's intriguing design, was pure imagination fuel for many fans who wondered who these warriors were and what happened between them and the Jedi.

During the production of the second season of *Star Wars: The Clone Wars*, George Lucas decided it was time to explore the Mandalorian people and their culture. This led to TV series, books, and this collection that you are reading now.

This specially curated souvenir edition features interviews and articles including *The Clone Wars* supervising director Dave Filoni discussing the animated debut of the Mandalorians to coverage of the filming of the groundbreaking TV series, *The Mandalorian* and *The Book of Boba Fett*.

Also featured is an interview with the first actor to to don the armor onscreen, the much-missed Jeremy Bulloch, whose dedication and kindness to fans will always be remembered.

Jonathan

Jonathan Wilkins
Editor

TITAN EDITORIAL
Editor / Jonathan Wilkins
Group Editor / Jake Devine
Editorial Assistant / Ibraheem Kazi
Art Director / Oz Browne
Designer / David Colderley

LUCASFILM
Senior Editor / Brett Rector
Art Director / Troy Alders
Creative Director / Michael Siglain
Asset Management /
Chris Argyropoulos, Gabrielle Levenson,
Shahana Alam, Jackey Cabrera,
Elinor De La Torre, Bryce Pinkos,
Michael Trobiani, Sarah Williams
Story Group / Leland Chee, Pablo Hidalgo,
Emily Shkoukani, Phil Szostak,
and Kate Izquierdo

CONTRIBUTORS
Tricia Barr, Kristin Baver, S.T. Bende,
James Burns, Christopher Gates, Pat Jankiewicz,
John Kirk, Mark Newbold, Amy Ratcliffe,
Darren Scott, Jay Stobie, Bryan Young

SPECIAL THANKS TO
Lucy Goldsmith, Erich Schoeneweiss
at Random House, Holly McIntosh,
Joseph Taraborrelli, Andrea Towers and
Jim Nausedas at Marvel Comics, Lizzy Draeger,
Tracy Cannobbio and Lyn Cowen at Lucasfilm.
Kevin P. Pearl, Samantha Keane,
and Eugene Paraszczuk at Disney.

TITAN MAGAZINES
Production Controllers /
Caterina Falqui & Kelly Fenton
Production Manager / Jackie Flook
Sales & Circulation Manager / Steve Tothill
Marketing Coordinator / Lauren Noding
Publicity & Sales Coordinator / Alexandra Iciek
Publicity Manager / Will O'Mullane
Publicist / Caitlin Storer
Digital & Marketing Manager / Jo Teather
Head of Rights / Jenny Boyce
Head of Creative & Business Development /
Duncan Baizley
Publishing Director / Ricky Claydon
Publishing Director / John Dziewiatkowski
Group Operations Director / Alex Ruthen
Executive Vice President / Andrew Sumner
Publishers / Vivian Cheung & Nick Landau

DISTRIBUTION
U.S. Distribution / Penguin Random House
U.K. Distribution / MacMillon Distribution
Direct Sales Market / Diamond Comic
Distributors
General Enquiries / customerservice@
titanpublishingusa.com

Star Wars Insider Presents
The Mandalorian Collection is published by Titan
Magazines, a division of Titan Publishing Group Limited, 144
Southwark Street, London, SE1 0UP.

Printed in China.
For sale in the U.S., Canada, U.K., and Eire

ISBN: 9781787739994

Published by Titan Magazines
A division of Titan Publishing Group Ltd.,
144 Southwark Street, London SE1 0UP

Contents © 2023 Lucasfilm Ltd. & TM. All Rights Reserved
Titan Authorised User.4261

First Edition February 2024

10 9 8 7 6 5 4 3 2 1

Printed in China.

© 2023 Lucasfilm Ltd. and ™ All Rights Reserved.
Used Under Authorization.

Contents

THE ART OF MANDA

THE MANDALORIANS' DEBUT IN STAR WARS: THE CLONE WARS HAS PROVED TO BE A HUGE TALKING POINT FOR FANS OF THE SAGA. WHEN LUCASFILM HELD A SPECIAL SCREENING OF "THE MANDALORE PLOT" FOR FANS, SUPERVISING DIRECTOR DAVE FILONI TOOK TIME TO TALK ABOUT THE DESIGN CHOICES MADE ON THE SHOW.

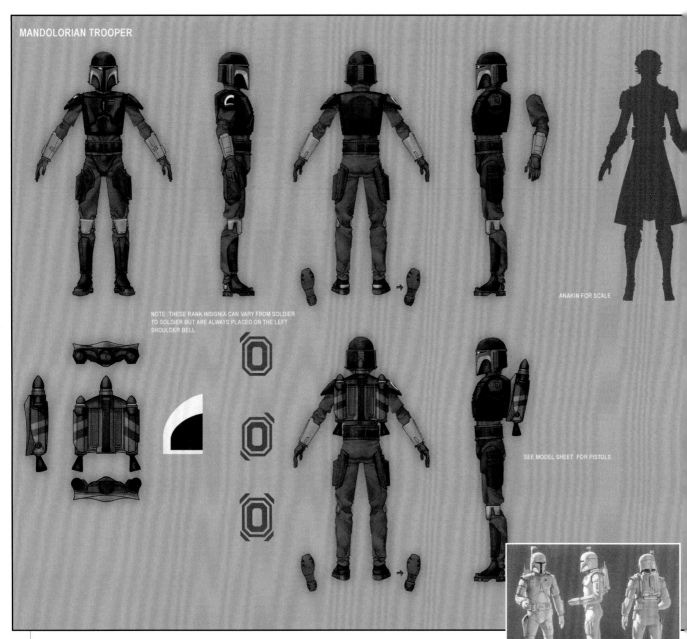

NOTE: THESE RANK INSIGNIA CAN VARY FROM SOLDIER TO SOLDIER BUT ARE ALWAYS PLACED ON THE LEFT SHOULDER BELL

ANAKIN FOR SCALE

SEE MODEL SHEET FOR PISTOLS

THE MANDALORIANS

Dave Filoni

"George Lucas' original idea was that the Mandalorians were super-commandos, a precursor to the stormtroopers from the Clone Wars era. You could see that in all of Ralph McQuarrie and Joe Johnston's early sketches of Mandalorians, so George really was taking us back to that original root, now that he had The Clone Wars as a series to actually tell this story and use them as super-commandos.

"If they were colored white, they would be like the clones, so George wanted them to be clad in blue and black. We had the old Boba Fett symbol on Pre Vizsla's back and I said, "No." I wanted the Death Watch symbol, the correct symbol." They don't have gadgetry at this stage. That's someplace for them to go to resemble more of what writer Haden Blackman had with his original Death Watch in the Dark Horse Comics.

'The helmet that we had designed was based much more on Boba's actual proportions. It's pretty squat if you look at the picture, very boxy. But Kilian Plunkett [Star Wars: The Clone Wars concept artist] had a really good idea that we should stretch it out a little bit to make it a little bit funkier, a little longer."

Above: The all-new Mandalorians, as seen in Star Wars: The Clone Wars. Right: These Boba Fett concept images, created by Ralph McQuarrie and Joe Johnston for The Empire Strikes Back, provided inspiration for the production team.

PRE VIZSLA

Dave Filoni

"For Pre Vizsla, we just wanted something that called him out as the leader. We took the range finder off his helmet. It was an effort to make Boba Fett cooler, and Jango cooler, and Rex cooler. I didn't want kids to be confused, because he would really look like Rex with a range finder. So we simplified it down; we distilled the helmet to its essence, and a trident is always a good symbol. When we did that we didn't know about the Death Watch logo. I found that one day going through some material and thought, *Wow, that's a coincidence.*

When you have a leader, it's always important that he stands out from everybody else. For the clone commanders, we can get into any military reason we would like as to why they look like they do. The reality is they look like they do so that kids know that they're the ones in charge. It's like the question of why does that one sandtrooper have an orange pauldron? You can create all kinds of lore about that, but the reality is cinematically, you know that this is the guy who calls the shots. "

Left: Pre Vizsla, armed and extremely dangerous! Right: Concept art for his armor. Below: Armor-free, but still deadly!

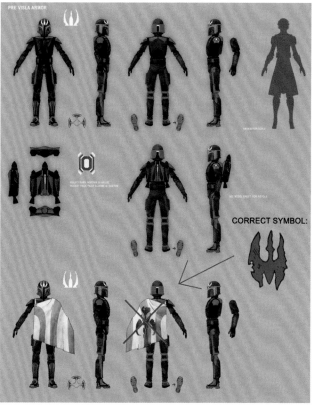

CORRECT SYMBOL:

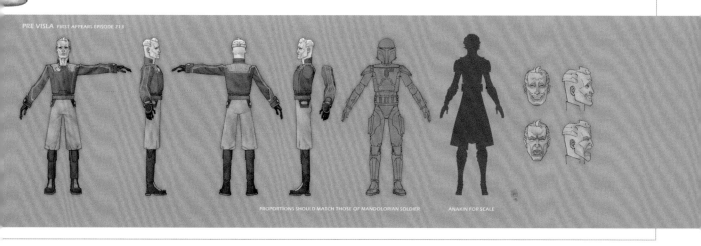

THE DUCHESS SATINE

Dave Filoni

"I thought it would be great to get a blonde girl in *Star Wars*! Satine's genesis as a look came from an abandoned Padmé design Iain McCaig had done for *The Phantom Menace*. Every now and then when we have a story pitch, George will take images out of this old binder he has, and he'll hand it over, and he'll say, 'This is Satine.' I'll say, 'Well it looks like an old abandoned Padmé design,' and he'll say, 'Yeah, but now it's Satine.' I likened her to Cate Blanchett."

Left and below: Duchess Satine, *Star Wars'* first blonde bombshell! Right: Ian McCaig's dazzling Padmé art that was used 10 years later!

SATINE COSTUME 2   08/04 FIRST APPEARS EPISODE 213

DUCHESS SATINE

MANDALORE

Dave Filoni

One of the first things George said when we started discussing these episodes was that Mandalore was going to be a large desolate planet of white sand with these cube-like buildings on it. At one point I didn't even have the buildings quite square enough. The big capital city didn't look enough like a giant city, so we made it a dome with little cubes on it, but it's kind of a Moebius-influenced design, very desolate and barren. It's all that remains after the wars have happened and everything has been laid to waste. George also wanted to see through layers of glass. You can see characters underneath and above the glass.

"I talked to Kilian Plunkett about having the look of the Boba armor, kind of emblematic, in all the windows and all the designs, so you get those shapes that show up like a piece of his armor. That idea—that they are warriors—is embedded in the very architecture, because it's strong."

Left: The stunning landscapes of Mandalore. Below and right: Sketches of Mandalorian citizens.

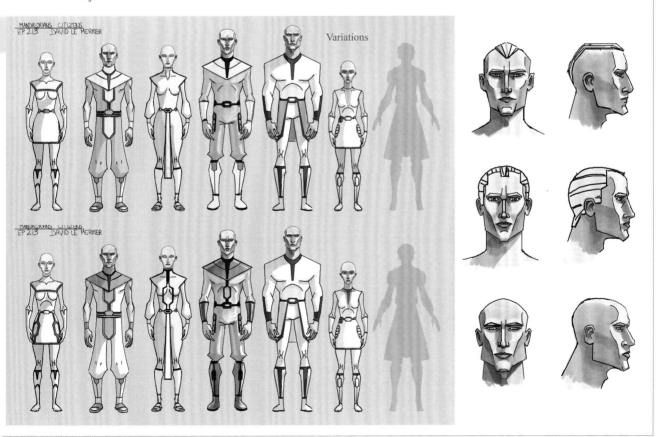

MANDALORIAN SHIPS

Dave Filoni

"I always liked *Star Wars* ships that had some kind of re-orienting wing. When Boba Fett's ship took off and it was different in the air than it was on the ground, I was like: Oh, that's so cool! And the B-wing has little wings, and it's getting rotated. I love that stuff! So we had this weird orienting wing, where it can fly sideways and straight up and down, and when it lands its wings tilt right up."

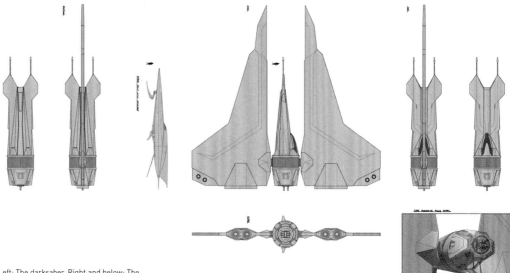

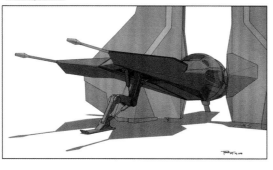

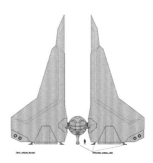

Left: The darksaber. Right and below: The Mandalorians' preferred mode of transport.

THE DARKSABER

Dave Filoni

"The darksaber carried by Pre Vizsla was originally a vibroblade. Initially there was no sword fight with Pre Vizsla in the script. He had to have a fight, and he had to have a saber, but he couldn't have a lightsaber because I know it's a contentious thing when any character who is not a Jedi carries a lightbsaber.

"George watched it and said, "No way. There's no way that there would be a weapon shaped like a sword that could counter a lightsaber blade. If you do that, a lightsaber isn't special, and then why wouldn't the Jedi also be using those things? It doesn't make any sense."

He later worked it out that he wanted it to be a darksaber, and it would have a black blade with a white edge. George said that the back-story was that the darksaber was taken from the Jedi Temple during the days of the Old Republic. I think it's unique and it's going to make an awesome EFX replica darksaber. I promised Jon Favreau (Pre Vizsla) as soon as they make one he gets one, so I hope they do!"

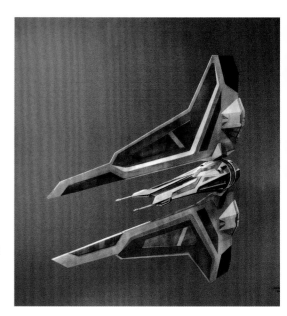

This article was based on a live interview conducted with Dave Filoni by Pablo Hidalgo, content manager of starwars.com

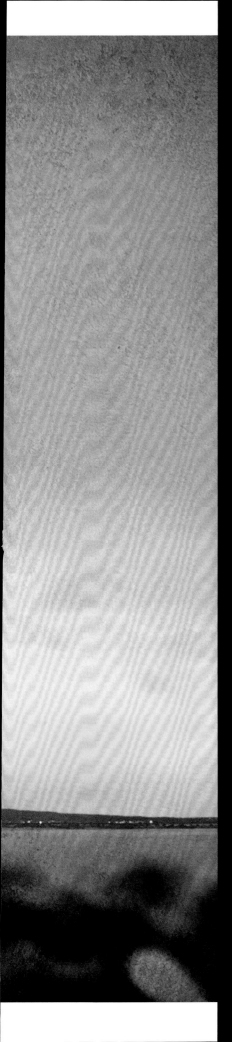

STAR WARS

THE

MANDALORIAN

Season One Companion

The Mandalorian became an instant hit when it landed on Disney+ in 2019. This is a guide to the episodes that introduced audiences to the Mandalorian and his adventures.

WORDS: KRISTIN BAVER

F or two seasons now, the taciturn armored warrior known to his friends as Mando, along with his pint-sized green companion the Child, have captivated viewers of *The Mandalorian* on Disney+.

Following the week-by-week release of its first season, the Jon Favreau and Dave Filoni-led series took home a bounty of seven Primetime Creative Arts Emmy Awards, was nominated for Outstanding Drama Series at the 72nd Primetime Emmy Awards, and earned praise from critics and fans alike. But the creators were just getting started.

Anchored by all-new characters finding their way in an era of *Star Wars* storytelling, some five years after the fall of the Empire, at its emotional core *The Mandalorian* is the story of Din Djarin grappling to reconcile his belief in the ideological creed under which he was raised, the bounty-hunter's code that had allowed him to support himself, and his willingness to risk it all to protect a young foundling who is far from helpless but certainly needs his protection.

As we await *The Book of Boba Fett* and *The Mandalorian*'s third season, *Star Wars Insider* presents our exclusive two-part exploration of the first 16 chapters of the groundbreaking Disney+ series.

TRIVIA

Assassin droid IG-11 looks a lot like the bounty hunter IG-88, first seen in *Star Wars: The Empire Strikes Back* (1980). To help differentiate between the two, IG-11 was given a distinctive double bandolier and claw-like hands for grasping a pair of blasters.

CHAPTER 2
The Child

Directed by Rick Famuyiwa
Written by Jon Favreau
First Airdate: November 15, 2019
After acquiring the Child, the Mandalorian must outwit other hunters and strike a deal with scavengers to escape from Arvala-7.

The second chapter hinted at the Child's Force abilities and planted the seeds of an unexpected attachment blossoming between the stoic helmeted hero and his small charge. Using far less dialogue than other episodes in the season, Famuyiwa's storytelling focused on the solitary struggle of the Mandalorian with stunning visuals punctuated by Ludwig Göransson's evocative score. Featuring a second appearance from Nick Nolte as the voice of Kuiil, the Mandalorian was forced to admit that sometimes even he needed a helping hand.

CHAPTER 1
The Mandalorian

Directed by Dave Filoni
Written by Jon Favreau
First Airdate: November 12, 2019
In the series premiere, the masked warrior known as the Mandalorian is hired for a secret bounty-hunting job to secure a mysterious asset for a wealthy client.

In the closing moments of the gritty *Star Wars* series' debut episode, viewers were surprised by the introduction of the Child, a nameless alien hailing from the same species as beloved Jedi Master Yoda.

In addition to Pedro Pascal starring as the eponymous hired gun, the series featured a legion of cameo appearances and supporting cast members starting off with Carl Weathers as Greef Karga, Werner Herzog as the Client, Nick Nolte as the voice of Kuiil, and Taika Waititi as the suicidal bounty hunting droid IG-11.

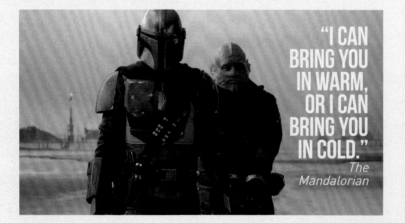

"I CAN BRING YOU IN WARM, OR I CAN BRING YOU IN COLD."
The Mandalorian

Chapter 2 director Rick Famuyiwa.

TALES FROM THE CUTTING EDGE

Season One of *The Mandalorian* introduced audiences to a slew of fascinating new characters, in a previously unexplored *Star Wars* era, but the creators of the series were determined to produce a show that looked and felt authentic to the galaxy far, far away.

To do so, they utilized cutting edge Stagecraft technology, shooting an apparently vast expanse of locations inside a single, enclosed set comprised of high-definition LED screens known as the Volume. Flawless digital graphics combined with traditionally made costumes and props, alongside practical effects, to recreate the "used world" look of the *Star Wars* galaxy—a nod to the model makers, puppeteers, and performers who made the original trilogy come alive.

CHAPTER 3
The Sin

Directed by Deborah Chow
Written by Jon Favreau
First Airdate: November 22, 2019
Safely back on Nevarro, the Mandalorian delivers on the job and receives his reward—a camtono case of beskar. But a sudden change of heart leads him into danger.

Introducing some backstory for the lead character, a sequence of cinematic flashbacks detailed a harrowing encounter the young Mando had with a super battle droid on the day he became a foundling. Intercut with shots of the Armorer forging new beskar armor for Mando, the scene was a poignant introduction that explained the eponymous character's lasting dislike for droids, and helped to cement his connection with the Child. It also went a long way to showing why he would risk everything to protect the youngling.

Guest actor Omin Abtahi brought the sniveling Dr. Pershing to life, while Emily Swallow returned as the Armorer.

Chapter 3 director Deborah Chow with Pedro Pascal as the Mandalorain.

"SUCH A LARGE BOUNTY FOR SUCH A SMALL PACKAGE."
The Client (Werner herzog)

CHAPTER 4
Sanctuary

Directed by Bryce Dallas Howard
Written by Jon Favreau
First Airdate: November 29, 2019
In an attempt to lay low and hide from those he's crossed, the Mandalorian and the Child fly to Sorgan where they find locals badly in need of protection.

In her directorial debut for the series, Bryce Dallas Howard paid homage to the classic Akira Kurosawa film *Seven Samurai* (1954), in a story that pitted a village of farmers (with help from a couple of hired fighters) against a band of thieves who regularly raided their harvest. The episode marked the first appearance of Gina Carano as Cara Dune, an ex-rebel shocktrooper who had no love for what was left of the Empire. The former mixed martial artist performed her own stunt work, and her sporting background helped inform the physicality of the role.

TRIVIA
Director Bryce Dallas Howard uses film history to anchor her contemporary storytelling, and her episode was influenced by the films of legendary Japanese director Akira Kurosawa.
As a child, Howard was lucky to meet Kurosawa, when her father—*Solo: A Star Wars Story* (2018) director Ron Howard—was invited to dine with him and brought her along.

Chapter 4 director Bryce Dallas Howard.

TRIVIA

NEVARRO
The city of Nevarro shares a link with Batuu, the *Star Wars*: Galaxy's Edge planet at Walt Disney World Resort and Disneyland Resort. For both worlds, designers took inspirational cues from the architecture of Morocco in North Africa, and buildings and bazaars in the Middle East.

DROID TRIO
Peli Motto's trio of pit droids are relics from the prequel era, first seen in *Star Wars: The Phantom Menace* (1999), servicing podracers (clumsily and sometimes fatally) during the Boonta Eve Classic at Mos Espa's Grand Arena.

FROG LADY
Hidden among the Mos Eisley Cantina patrons in Chapter 5, you can spot two characters who will play a more prominent role in Season 2: Dr. Mandible and the alien known as Frog Lady (played by Kuiil performer Misty Rosas).

CHAPTER 5
The Gunslinger

Directed and Written by Dave Filoni
First Airdate: December 6, 2019
A fuel leak forces the Mandalorian to seek refuge, repairs, and employment on Tatooine.

This story took viewers back to where it all began in 1977: the blistering desert planet of Tatooine. Familiar sights included the bustling spaceport of Mos Eisley and its infamous Cantina, more than a few sandy dunes, a dewback, and a couple of native Tusken Raiders encountered by Mando in the depths of the Dune Sea.

Instead of portraying the Tuskens as savages, the story introduced a form of sign language that enabled Mando to communicate with them, developed with the help of Troy Kotsur, one of the Tusken actors who is hearing impaired. The episode also included cameo appearances from Amy Sedaris as Peli Motto, the gruff proprietor of Docking Bay 3-5; Jake Cannavale as bounty hunting-hopeful Toro Calican; and Ming-Na Wen as elite assassin Fennec Shand. Special guest Mark Hamill provided the voice for the cantina's EV-series droid bartender.

CHAPTER 6
The Prisoner

Directed by Rick Famuyiwa
Written by Rick Famuyiwa
and Christopher Yost
First Airdate: December 13, 2019
Desperate to make some credits,
the Mandalorian tracks down an old
colleague and agrees to undertake
a dangerous mission.

Chapter 6 had more than its
fair share of famous guest stars,
including Mark Boone Jr. as Ranzar
Malk, Bill Burr as Migs Mayfeld,
Richard Ayoade as the voice of
Zero, Natalia Tena as Xi'an, Ismael
Cruz Cordova as Qin, and Clancy
Brown as Burg. However, several
smaller roles featured cameo
appearances by some familiar *Star
Wars* names, if not faces. Matt
Lanter (interviewed in this issue),
who voiced Anakin Skywalker in
Star Wars: The Clone Wars (2008-
2014, 2020), played New Republic
prison guard Davan, while three
directors from the series—Deborah
Chow, Rick Famuyiwa, and Dave
Filoni— turned up as a trio of New
Republic X-wing pilots.

CHAPTER 7
The Reckoning

Directed by Deborah Chow
Written by Jon Favreau
First Airdate: December 18, 2019
The Mandalorian and Greef Karga cut a
deal with a plan to take out the Imperial
Client who originally put the bounty on
the Child, and clear Mando's name with
the Bounty Hunters Guild.

As the stakes grew at the tail end of
Season One, key characters reunited
to defend the Child, including the
surprise return of IG-11, once again
voiced by Taika Waititi. Although
Mando shot the assassin droid at point-
blank range in the series opener, we
learned that it had been resurrected by
the Ugnaught Kuiil, and reprogrammed
to serve and protect.
    Giancarlo Esposito also
made his unforgettable
entrance in the series,
as the fearsome
Moff Gideon.

TRIVIA

Chapter 7 includes
the first live-action
appearance of an
Imperial Troop
Transport. Longtime
fans began playing
with a toy version of
the vehicle in the late
1970s, but it didn't
make it on screen
until it appeared
several times in
Star Wars Rebels
(2014-2018).

TRIVIA

ALDERAAN

Cara Dune's homeworld of Alderaan is a callback to the original *Star Wars* hero, Princess Leia Organa, who was adopted as a baby by the queen of Alderaan and watched as the world was annihilated by the Empire's first Death Star. With a single mention of that world, longtime fans instantly got a sense of all that Dune had lost.

MOS EISLEY

When the Mandalorian visits the Mos Eisley Cantina, it's a very different place to our first visit to the watering hole in *Star Wars: A New Hope* (1977). For one thing, instead of the grizzled bartender Wuher slinging drinks, the barkeep is now a droid. As you may recall, the establishment didn't even serve droid-kind back then.

Designers scoured archive film footage and behind-the-scenes imagery to faithfully recreate every shadowy corner of the Cantina, including the sign hanging over the main entrance. For the latter, Roger Christian—the set designer on *A New Hope*—was the only person who had a clear photographic reference of the original sign for them to work from.

DR. PERSHING

Dr. Pershing's uniform contains a clue as to his intentions with the Child. The symbol on his sleeve is strikingly similar to the Kaminoan cloning facility emblem seen on the uniforms of a legion of clone cadets still in training in *Star Wars: Attack of the Clones* (2002).

"I WOULD GLADLY BREAK ANY PROMISE AND WATCH YOU DIE AT MY HAND."
Moff Gideon (giancarlo esposito)

CHAPTER 8
Redemption

Directed by Taika Waititi / Written by Jon Favreau
First Airdate: December 27, 2019
The Mandalorian and his friends must face a legion of stormtroopers, deadly death troopers, and defy the cold-hearted Moff Gideon, as they fight to defend the Child.

Chapter 8 marked the first time the Mandalorian's true name, Din Djarin, was spoken in the series. It was also the first time we saw star Pedro Pascal's face on screen, revealed to viewers (and IG-11) after the character was mortally wounded.

Pulling together story threads from preceding chapters, the season finale finally revealed the full story of Din's tragic childhood, and set him on the quest that went on to dominate the second season. As a clan of two with the Child, a mudhorn signet symbolizing their bond, the Mandalorian accepted his duty of care towards the youngling, vowing to reunite it with its own kind—the Jedi.

Taika Waititi took the director's chair for the blistering season finale.

THE
MANDALORIAN

The *Star Wars* Archive

The behind-the-scenes story of a galaxy far, far away....

THE COLDEST OF COLD OPENS

Chapter 1 of *The Mandalorian* debuted on Disney+ on November 12, 2019, with a pre-titles sequence that neatly defined what we should expect from the show's lead character, using a narrative technique known as a "cold open," which dropped viewers straight into the adventure.

That the action took place on an ice planet (Pagodon), with the first few scenes seemingly filmed on a chilly glacier, the opening couldn't have been much colder. The bounty hunter's capture of the Mythrol followed by an almost deadly encounter with a ravanak was the epitome of cool, and introduced fans to the resourceful if a little galaxy-weary mercenary whose name we wouldn't learn until the final episode of the first season. ▶

01 Director Dave Filoni
   (center right) talking
   to actors Brian
   Posehn (speeder
   Pilot) and Horatio
   Sanz (the Mythrol)
   on the ice-planet set.

02 Ice planet concept art
   by Nick Gindraux.

03 Series creator Jon
   Favreau (left) with
   Brian Posehn (right)
   as the speeder Pilot.

03

04

04 Director of Photography Greig Fraser (left) lining up the opening shot of Chapter 1 of *The Mandalorian* (2019 –).

05 Filming Din Djarin's arrival at the ice planet outpost on Industrial Light & Magic's StageCraft LED volume.

06 (Left to right) 1st assistant director Kim Richards, Jon Favreau, Greig Fraser, and Dave Filoni discuss a shot with members of the crew, framed by the entrance to the ice planet public house.

07 Filming Take 1, Scene L101F, as indicated by the two clapperboards in this behind-the-scenes shot, one for each camera angle.

06

THE WHISTLE BLOWER

When Luke Skywalker and his friends entered Mos Eisley's Docking Bay 94 in *A New Hope* (1977), they were observed by a spy by the name of Garindan (pictured below), who reported their arrival to his Imperial paymasters.

He wasn't the only "whistle blowing" member of the Kubaz species, however, as we learned in *The Mandalorian*'s opening episode, where another Kubaz—the "Ferry-Man" (played by Chris Bartlett, and pictured above in concept art by Brian Matyas)—was seen using a wind instrument as a signal at the ice planet's speeder dock.

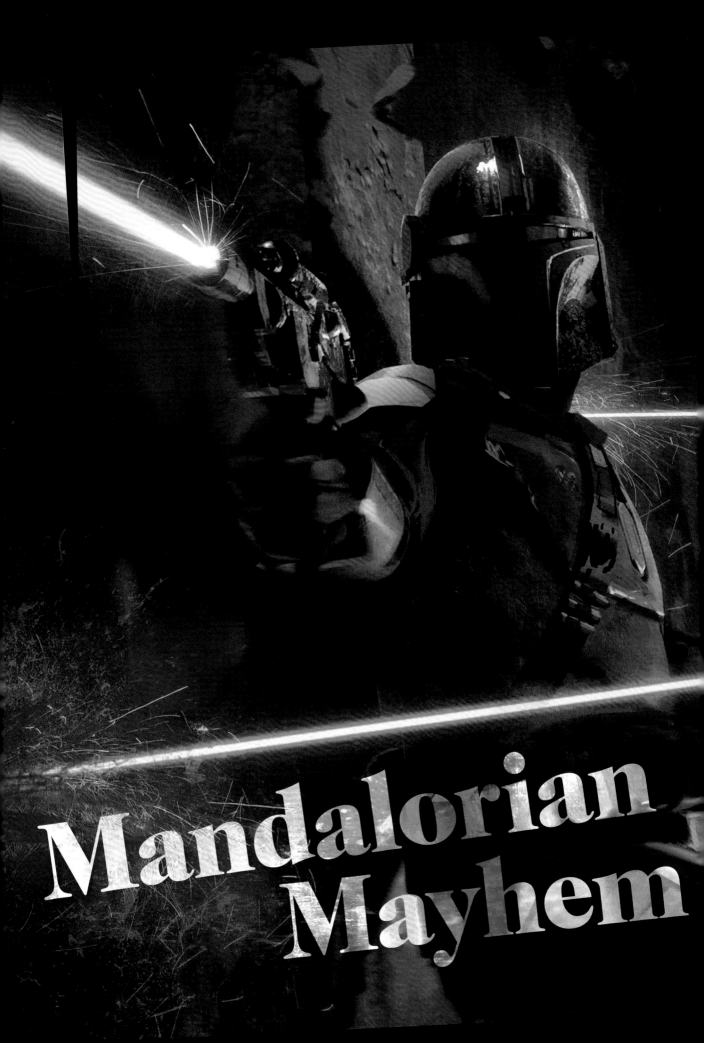

Insider's Top 10 brawls, fights, and fisticuffs from *The Mandalorian*!

WORDS: JAY STOBIE

T he Mandalorian (2019-present) has packed quite a punch in terms of storytelling, character development, and surprise reveals, and when combined with the show's unparalleled action sequences it's no surprise that the Disney+ series has turned out to be a big hitter for the streaming platform. The first sixteen chapters have also proven that bounty hunting isn't just a complicated profession, it's also a physically dangerous one too, as this look back at our favorite fight scenes from the first two seasons proves.

10

Dealing with Death Troopers

■ Trapped in a building on Nevarro with Moff Gideon's Imperial forces gathered outside, Din Djarin and his allies seemed destined for capture—or worse! IG-11, reprogrammed as a nurse droid yet still capable of calling upon his assassin past, swooped in on a speeder bike to provide Djarin with an opening to strike back. Din came out blasting, dispatching two stormtroopers before encountering a duo of death troopers, the elite soldiers who originally made their fearsome debut in *Rogue One: A Star Wars Story* (2016). In a flash of fists, the bounty hunter bested the two assailants, demonstrating that not even Gideon's toughest troops could handle a well-trained Mandalorian.

09

Mando Hates Droids

■ In the process of infiltrating a New Republic prison ship, Din Djarin and a team of mercenaries ran afoul of the security droids who patrolled the vessel's hallways. Unbeknownst to his compatriots, Djarin decided to flank the quartet of droids and surprise them with a furious assault that saw him deploy his full arsenal—vibroblade, blaster pistol, flamethrower, whipcord, and bare hands—against the automated New Republic guards. Djarin dismantled his opponents with a graceful brutality, possibly finding motivation from his memory of losing his parents to Separatist droids during the Clone Wars. The performance even dazzled his temporary compatriots, who watched in awe as the bounty hunter made "easy" work of the droids.

SPECIAL MOVES
CLASH OF THE KLATOOINIANS

In an effort to protect Sorgan's farmers, Din Djarin chose to bait a band of Klatooinian raiders into a trap that would discourage the group from pillaging a remote village. After engaging in hand-to-hand combat with the Klatooinian camp's guards, Djarin headed for home, where he courageously charged an AT-ST and destroyed the walker with one of his signature explosive devices.

08

A Backroom Battle

■ Din Djarin expected to encounter trouble wherever he went, particularly when traveling through a barren city at night on the way to an underground fighting den filled with criminals and other malicious characters. On the hunt for other Mandalorians, the beskar-clad hunter attempted to bargain with Gor Koresh for helpful information, but the deceitful entrepreneur had another idea in mind, electing to spring a trap on our intrepid hero. Of course, Djarin was well prepared, taking down the first wave of enemies with "whistling birds" and evading a ferocious dive from a muscular Gamorrean.

In a presentation of well-honed skill and brute strength, Djarin utilized his valuable beskar armor to block strikes,

even finding a way to deploy his helmet as an offensive weapon. With the flick of a wrist, Mando subdued two Zabraks with his vibroblade before turning his attention to a fleeing Gor Koresh. Captured by a whipcord, the hostile leader immediately sought to become Din Djarin's newest best friend, offering up the location of a Mandalorian on Tatooine. Djarin stayed true to his word when he opted not to kill Gor Koresh by his own hand, but the local wildlife was not nearly as forgiving.

commander elected to scupper the vessel rather than permit its cargo to be stolen. Pinned down by blaster fire with precious time until impact ticking away, Djarin valiantly charged the well-armed stormtroopers who guarded the bridge, relying on his beskar to protect him from volleys of lethal energy. At the last second, Mando tossed two charges at his foes and cleared the way for his allies to secure control of the ship.

07

Acquiring a Cruiser

■ You might think that boarding an Imperial starship filled with well-armed stormtroopers would land higher up on our list, and you would have good

reason to wonder why it does not rank at the very top. As impressive as this heist was, Din Djarin benefited from the help of three fellow Mandalorians on this mission. Nevertheless, the cadre was still heavily outnumbered by their Imperial counterparts. Bo-Katan Kryze, Koska Reeves, Axe Woves, and Djarin flew up to the *Gozanti*-class cruiser with their jetpacks and slugged their way through several corridors of stormtroopers.

Once the Remnant forces knew that the "pirates" were actually Mandalorians and defeat was inevitable, the ship's

06

The Jawa Chase

■ Fresh off defending his recently acquired asset—the child, Grogu—from Trandoshan bounty hunters, Din Djarin encountered the discouraging sight of Jawas dismantling his precious *Razor Crest* for parts. After an initial barrage from his rifle disintegrated several Jawas, the scavengers quickly mounted up to make a getaway in their massive sandcrawler. Failing to damage the behemoth from long-range, Djarin pursued the vehicle on foot until he could grab hold of its exterior plating.

Faced with a treacherous climb and many angry Jawas, either of which could send him plummeting from the side of the speeding crawler, Din Djarin battled his way up the vehicle's hull, dodging rocky crevices and falling debris along the way. Upon finally reaching the top of his ascent, Mando was greeted by a wall of Jawas whose weapons stunned the bounty hunter and sent him crashing to the muddy ground far below. Despite his unsuccessful bid to regain equipment from the *Razor Crest*, the sheer challenge of the chase made Din Djarin's efforts that much more spectacular, even though this is one of the few times he failed in his mission.

05

Allying with IG-11

■ Have we mentioned that Din Djarin hates droids? En route to take custody of an unknown target, the bounty hunter was dismayed to see an IG unit approach the kidnappers' encampment to nab the bounty for itself. IG-11's blaster bolts struck their marks with stunning accuracy, but the droid ultimately acquiesced to Djarin's request to split the reward and improve their odds by working together. In the midst of an intense firefight, the guards trapped the two bounty hunters and brought out a large blaster cannon. This error worked in Djarin's favor, as he commandeered the weapon to wipe out the rest of the thieves.

Though this confrontation was more of a shootout than a brawl, it highlighted Djarin's capacity to look beyond his antagonism toward droids and team up with one for a common goal. Considering the horrors he had faced as a child, this battle demonstrated the bounty hunter's mental courage, a trait which allowed him to weather the trauma of his youth. Admittedly, Djarin did end up shooting IG-11, but, in all fairness, the droid was about to do the same to Grogu at the time.

04

Melee with a Moff

■ The nefarious Moff Gideon held Grogu (one of the few beings in the galaxy with whom Din Djarin had truly bonded) captive aboard his *Arquitens*-class flagship. The Imperial holdout stood as the only enemy in the way of retrieving Din Djarin's ward, yet the bounty hunter offered to let Gideon go—so long as he safely returned the child. As one would anticipate, Gideon drew the Darksaber as soon as Djarin's back was turned, igniting an intense scrape that seemed to be as personal as it was perilous.

Mando's armor withstood the Darksaber's initial salvos before the bounty hunter called upon his beskar staff's ability to block the energy blade. The two parried back and forth, each man trading hits and searching for the upper hand. Djarin showcased a majestic move, kicking his staff in a high arc to swing at Gideon. As the fight progressed, he managed to land enough blows to incapacitate the Moff, securing both victory and Grogu's freedom… as well as the Darksaber, and with it the right to rule Mandalore! Din Djarin achieved perhaps his greatest deed on one of the handful of occasions where he faced an adversary in one-on-one combat.

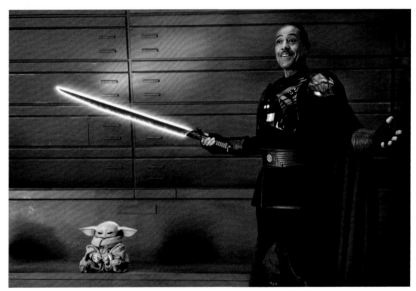

SPECIAL MOVES
BRAINS OVER BRAWN

Fresh off helping Cobb Vanth vanquish a krayt dragon, Din Djarin and Grogu were enjoying a leisurely speeder ride back to Mos Eisley until a gang of thieves sprung an unfortunate ambush. Outnumbered four-to-one, Djarin dodged blaster bolts and bladed weapons to subdue his first three opponents, but the fourth grabbed Grogu. The bounty hunter used his wits against his final foe, letting his jetpack to drop the last bandit from a treacherous height.

03

The Dark Trooper Disturbance

■ Although Djarin's unexpected friendship with IG-11 significantly improved his perception of droids, Moff Gideon's platoon of fully automated dark troopers focused all their efforts on destroying the Imperial's rivals, ultimately providing the bounty hunter with one of his fiercest fights to date. As the droids prepared to exit their alcoves,

he managed to seal all but one of them in their storage bay. However, a single dark trooper represented a formidable hurdle to overcome, as its exterior was impervious to blaster fire, whistling birds, and even Mando's trusted flamethrower.

The hefty droid overpowered the bounty hunter, punching Djarin's head into the wall. Only his beskar helmet protected Djarin from a swift defeat, keeping our hero alive long enough to

see the dark trooper's comrades doing their best to break through the blast doors. Unable to win through sheer physical fortitude, Din drew upon his intellect, stabbing his beskar staff through the vulnerable underside of the droid's head. The maneuver granted Djarin just enough time to eject the remaining dark troopers into space, supplying himself with a brief respite before their unanticipated return.

02

Trials on the Transport

■ Disguised as Imperial transport troopers in order to enter a top-secret refinery, Din Djarin and Migs Mayfeld were dismayed to witness marauders jump onto their vehicle and try to detonate its cargo. Mando made his way to the roof to fend off the interlopers, but he quickly realized that his disguise robbed him of the benefit of his beskar. As the bounty

hunter blocked a strike from one of the pirates, his less-than-adequate Imperial armor crumbled where his beskar would have maintained its integrity. Regardless of this unexpected disadvantage, Djarin expertly fought wave after wave of the attackers, certifying that his reputation as a warrior was not simply a byproduct of his impenetrable beskar suit.

01

Run-in with the Remnant

■ When Din Djarin decided to betray the code of his guild to rescue Grogu from the Client's clutches, he made enemies of both the Imperial Remnant stormtroopers and the bounty hunters who operated out of Nevarro. To save Grogu from the Remnant and evade the mercenaries who pursued him, Djarin conducted a master class in

the warrior ways of his people. From his explosive charges and whipcord to his vibroblade and flamethrower, Djarin pulled out all the stops to infiltrate the Client's facility, before taking out a small squad of stormtroopers with his whistling birds.

Djarin then had to weather weapons fire from Greef Karga and other guild members, forging a path with his own blaster pistol and rifle. Thankfully, when the hunters had him cornered and hope was beginning to fade, the rest of his covert arrived to even the odds and enable his escape. This engagement not only set the stage for Din Djarin's familial connection to Grogu, it also underscored what Mandalorians could accomplish, both as self-reliant individuals and as a unified force. Though Djarin ultimately needed help on this mission, it was only natural that it came from his Mandalorian brothers and sisters. Why? Well, there's only one answer to that question: This is the way. 🐗

SPECIAL MOVES
BESKAR VERSUS THE BLADE

While brief, the scuffle between Din Djarin and Ahsoka Tano in the forest on Corvus gave us our first live-action look at a face-off between a Mandalorian and a Jedi. Beskar armor blocked lightsaber strikes and Tano outmaneuvered Djarin's flamethrower in a dazzling display as the two highly trained combatants battled for supremacy. Luckily, the pair quickly realized they were on the same side.

The *Star Wars* Archive

The behind-the-scenes story of a galaxy far, far away....

SHARP AS A *RAZOR*

As immediately iconic as any of the *Star Wars* starships that came before, the design for the *Razor Crest* was an instant hit when it was first unveiled during a special preview panel for *The Mandalorian* (2019 -) at Celebration 2019.

Designed by design supervisor Ryan Church, many shots of the vessel in flight made use of a practical miniature model captured using traditional motion control techniques, on a rig built by effects veteran John Knoll. Large exterior sections of the ship, including the cockpit, the rear access ramp, and side entrance hatches, were built as separate set pieces for filming live-action scenes on the Volume.

02

03

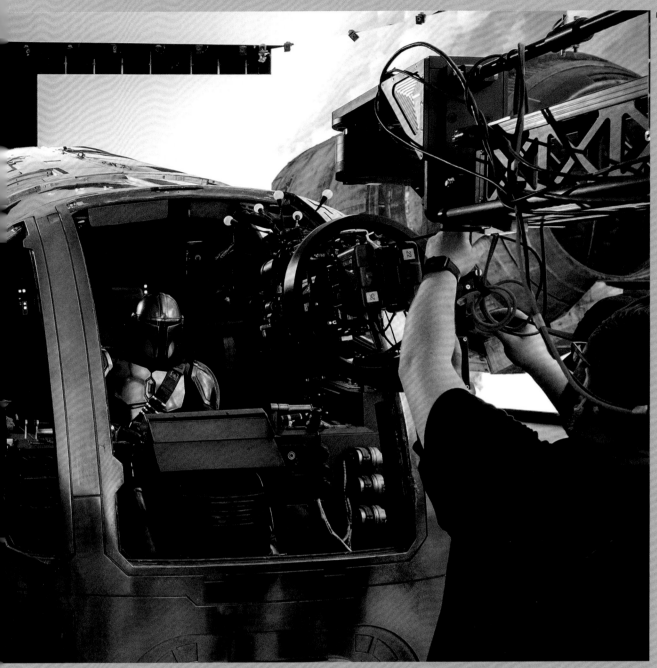

01 The crew film the Mandalorian at the controls of the *Razor Crest* for Chapter 12, "The Siege."

02 *Razor Crest* concept art by Doug Chiang for Chapter 1, "The Mandalorian."

03 Shooting on the Volume allowed the production to film *Razor Crest* exterior shots in any locale, from deep space to a crash site in an icy cavern.

THE
MANDALORIAN

Pedro Pascal

The Mysterious Gunslinger

Who is the Mandalorian? *Insider* caught up
with Pedro Pascal shortly before the series premiered
on Disney+.

WORDS: BRYAN YOUNG

01

edro Pascal is no stranger to big franchises like *Star Wars*. Over the course of his career, the Chilean-born actor has appeared in TV shows such as *Buffy the Vampire Slayer* and *Game of Thrones*, and feature films such as *Kingsman: The Golden Circle* (2017). Most recently, he even landed the villainous role of Maxwell Lord in the upcoming *Wonder Woman 1984*, the sequel to 2017's smash hit film starring Gal Gadot. Now, he has stepped into a galaxy far, far away, taking on the title role of *The Mandalorian*, a mysterious character who says little and reveals even less.

Much like his character on the Disney+ *Star Wars* show, Pascal likes to present a taciturn image, especially when asked to spill the beans on the Mandalorian bounty hunter and his adventures. Who is the Mandalorian? Where

does he come from? What is he after? These questions drive both the storyline and Pascal. "Sometimes we're very much a mystery to ourselves," he reflects. "Our own identity is in the discovery of what you're capable of, or what your destiny is, or whether you will live for yourself or for others. It's very much a part of Jon Favreau's vision of the story, which is built upon the galaxy George Lucas introduced to all of us."

So, are we to believe that this bounty hunter might fight for something more than himself and a fistful of credits by the end of his assignment? Will there be more at stake for him than just the money? Pascal makes it clear those are questions that can only be answered by watching the show.

Inside The Armor

One thing Pascal is happy to talk about is his iconic costume, although he remains cagey about whether audiences will see the character remove

03

02

04

> ## "Our own identity is in the discovery of what you're capable of, or what your destiny is."

PROFILE
PEDRO PASCAL

Born in an era of political unrest in his native Chile, Jose Pedro Balmaceda Pascal relocated with his family to Denmark when he was still a baby, before the family moved to the U.S. and settled in Orange County, California. He studied acting at New York University's Tisch School of the Arts, and enjoyed an extensive stage career as an actor and director. Pascal appeared in numerous TV series, including an episode of *Buffy the Vampire Slayer* in 1999, before finding international fame as Oberyn Martell in *Game of Thrones* (2014), and as DEA agent Javier Peña in *Narcos* (2015-2017).

01 The Mandalorian (Pedro Pascal) with the mysterious Child.

02 Never removed in public, the inscrutable beskar mask of the Mandalorian.

03 Under attack, the resourceful Mandalorian won't let competitors stand in the way of securing his bounty.

04 The fateful first meeting between the Mandalorian and the Child.

his helmet during the course of the series. As cool as he knows it looks, the armor can be difficult to work with. "Nothing that looks that good is going to be easy to wear," Pascal admits. "You just have to surrender to that fact and focus on the story. Because the language of the character is strictly physical, negotiating his story—with *all* of the costume pieces—*is* his story, essentially. That's new to me. It's cool and very challenging."

Despite the fact that it caused the actor some physical pain at times, Pascal is quick to credit the costume designers who created the impressive outfit. "We talk about the characters and the filmmakers, and all the departments involved in making the whole piece, but to me the biggest stars, really, are the people who

work on the show, on every single detail of our costumes, of the sets, the special effects, the lighting," he says. "It's a humbling reminder to really respect the artwork that goes into building this world."

It's All About the Story

Mandalorian armor may not be the most comfortable apparel, but Pascal keeps his focus on his performance and staying true to the amazing storytelling set forth by executive producers Jon Favreau and Dave Filoni, for whom he has nothing but kind words. "Dave Filoni is very self-deprecating and humble," Pascal says. "But he's also extremely open. He has no agenda. You don't get that too often, especially with ▶

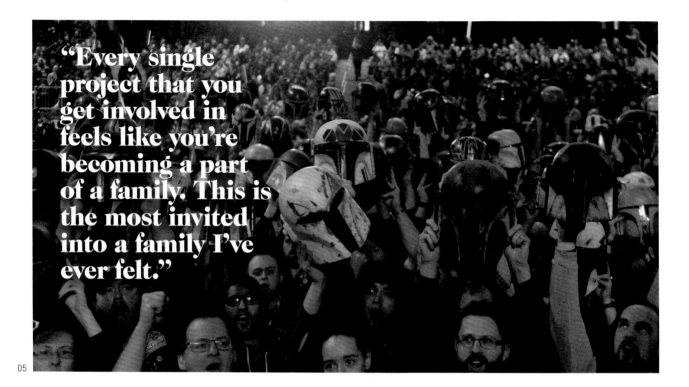

"Every single project that you get involved in feels like you're becoming a part of a family. This is the most invited into a family I've ever felt."

05

06

07

something that is as established as the *Star Wars* galaxy."

Pascal is equally as effusive about working with Favreau, and he feels the combination of the two creatives has made for a very special project. "To have people who are as excited about it as you are, and as the fans are—and as anyone who really wants a good story is—it makes for a really, really genuine, unique experience," he says.

For his part, Pascal feeds on that energy, crediting their enthusiasm for the *Star Wars* galaxy as a key part of what he has been able to bring to the role of the Mandalorian. "That energy helps you do the job," he explains. "It's a component that you don't count on, especially with *Star Wars*, because it can be very

05 Pascal describes the welcome he received at Celebration 2019 as a visceral "exchange of energy."

06 Dave Filoni and Pedro Pascal have fun with the audience at *Star Wars* Celebration.

07 Taking a bow at Celebration 2019: (Left to right) Jon Favreau, Dave Filoni, Pedro Pascal, Gina Carano, and Carl Weathers.

intimidating. It is a visual-effects experience, and an art-department experience. As a cast member, to have that kind of support to lift you into it, is such an essential component—more so than anything I've ever done."

Another pleasant surprise for Pascal has been how welcoming the wider world of *Star Wars* has been, including how the fans have embraced the series. "Every single project that you get involved with, it feels like you're becoming part of a family, but this is the most invited into a family I have ever felt," he shares. "It is an exchange of energy. It hit me like the back of a jet in Chicago at *Star Wars* Celebration. It's like a visceral realization. I have never felt anything like that." ☺

Enthusiastic, expressive, and with an infectious laugh and warm smile, it turns out that Emily Swallow is a very different person to the taciturn character she portrays in *The Mandalorian* (2019-present)—the enigmatic artisan, the Armorer.

Her face hidden beneath a horned helmet, the mysterious beskar blacksmith is an almost mystical figure in the hit Disney+ series, offering Din Djarin enigmatic advice when not forging tricked out kit and weaponry for the bounty hunter. Yet despite never showing her face, Swallow exudes an almost maternal warmth as the masked character.

"That's actually me under the helmet in all of my episodes," she says proudly. "Not being able to show my face was a wonderful challenge, because I had to communicate in other ways. I like to move around a lot, I'm very expressive—some call it mugging-to-camera—but as the Armorer I couldn't use any facial expressions at all. That was a challenge because I'm not always subtle (*laughs*). I found that all of the things that I thought would be limitations of working

in the helmet were, ultimately, strangely helpful to me."

A veteran of cult shows including *Supernatural* (2005-2020), in which she played the unstoppable Amara, *Seal Team* (2017-present), and *The Mentalist* (2013-2014), Swallow is a familiar face on television, so there is an irony in the fact that one of her best-known screen roles involves a head-to-toe costume, which she says became key to her portrayal of the stoic Mandalorian.

"The Armorer is somebody who exhibits a great deal of

trust," says Swallow. "She's very patient, she's not pushy, and I found it really helped me to be true to the character that I *had* to move simply and deliberately in the costume. I couldn't be looking down constantly to make sure my path was clear, so being able to trust that I wouldn't trip or fall became helpful to me in playing her. It was really fun for all of us who were wearing Mandalorian armor to learn the language of their movement together. It truly didn't feel like a hindrance because the more that we did it, the more confident we became."

The Power Of Zen

Despite appearing in only three episodes of *The Mandalorian*'s first season, the Armorer was a steady and dependable presence in all of her scenes. What aspects of the character most interested the actor?

"I wanted to show her authority, and that she had a great deal of confidence," Swallow explains. "And I wanted her to display a great deal of ease in showing it. She didn't strike me as being aggressive. In fact, one of the things that I remember most

▶

Fully Armed & Operational

Actor Emily Swallow talks exclusively to *Star Wars Insider* about the Zen-like inner strength of the Armorer, and how not tripping up on set helped her get into character.

WORDS: PAT JANKIEWICZ

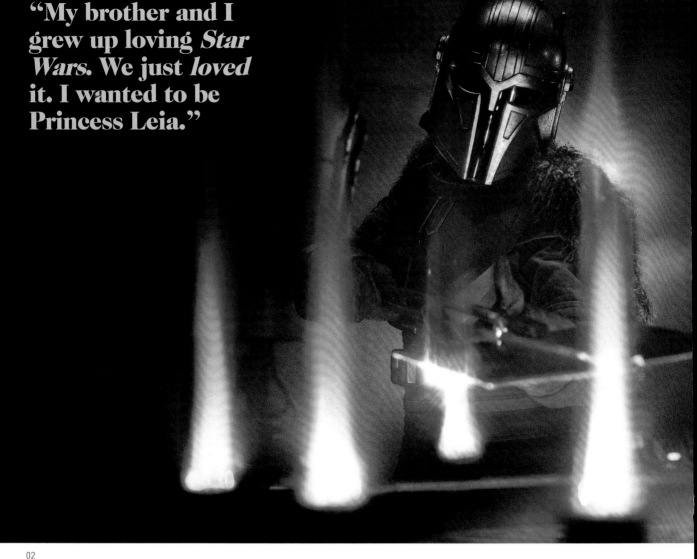

"My brother and I grew up loving *Star Wars*. We just *loved* it. I wanted to be Princess Leia."

02

03

02 The Armorer (Emily Swallow) forging beskar in her Nevarro workshop.

03 Director Deborah Chow (right) with Emily Swallow as the Armorer on the set of *The Mandalorian* Chapter 3, "The Sin."

like.' That was such a gift. It can be a trap for an actor if you're told that you're playing a character with a lot of power, as you tend to play it big because you think you have to show it—'I HAVE SO MUCH POWER!'" Swallow bellows in demonstration. "But the audience sees what you've done and thinks, 'That person is not very powerful at all!' If you're that powerful and in authority, there's no reason to push it. People just know.

"I'm very proud to be the Armorer," Swallow continues.

"She is so supportive of the people around her, which is such an admirable trait. It makes me want to be more like her. You really find the joy in being able to play somebody like that."

Talking of supportive people, Swallow has "a huge respect for executive producers Jon Favreau and Dave Filoni. Jon wanted to give *The Mandalorian* a classic *Star Wars* feel, which I love," says Swallow. "And thank goodness for Dave Filoni, who directed the pilot, because he knows everything there is to know about *Star Wars*. Deborah Chow (who directed Swallow in Chapter 3, 'The Sin') was great and made a big impression on me. Taika Waititi (the director of Chapter 8, 'Redemption') was so wild and so much fun, I had a blast! I am so lucky that I got to work with them!

"Deborah actually wound up influencing what I did as the

04

Armorer, and I didn't even realize it at the time," Swallow continues. "She was such a great and graceful presence on set—so confident, but so gentle—that I actually wound up borrowing some of that energy from her and putting it into the Armorer. She truly impressed me."

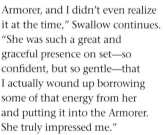

04 The Armorer (Swallow) sets Din Djarin (Pedro Pascal) on a new path, in Chapter 8, "Redemption."

The Swallow Saga

"My brother and I grew up loving *Star Wars*," the actor reminisces. "We just *loved* it. I wanted to be Princess Leia. I really thought we were true fans, but I've done some comic-book conventions since making the show and have met some *giant* fans. Women and girls have come up to me to tell me how much they love the Armorer. I'm always especially excited to meet tiny Armorers, little girls dressed like me! Oh, that just makes my heart swell!"

Swallow grew up in Jacksonville, Florida. Despite her later success, in her younger years a career in entertainment felt light years away. "As a kid I was always making up stories. I wanted to be an actor, but I didn't personally know any people who did that for a living, so it wasn't something I felt was within my

grasp." Instead, she started singing in a church choir. "I also did musicals and plays at school. When I went to college, I continued to perform— everything from Shakespeare (she won a Falstaff Award for Best Female Performer when she played Kate in *The Taming Of The Shrew*) to John Patrick Stanley—but I also majored in Middle Eastern Studies and Foreign Affairs."

With life in Hollywood a seemingly impossible dream, Swallow planned instead on going into the Foreign Service. "I studied at the University of Virginia, but all through college I split my time between my major and the drama department. I had a wonderful acting coach, Richard Warner, who told me, 'This is something that you have a gift for.' That is when I decided to become an actor, and I still consult with Richard on some roles. I have ▶

THE ARMORER HAS IT FIGURED

As a lifelong *Star Wars* fan, one of Emily Swallow's great joys in becoming a character in the saga has been being immortalized in plastic. "To be a *Star Wars* action figure? I mean, come on—it's so cool!" she enthuses. "My inner six year old jumps up and down with joy every time I get to sign one of those at comic-book conventions."

In addition to three Hasbro action figures (so far), the Armorer also has her own Funko Pop and a LEGO® minifigure. "I especially love the Hot Toys figure that has interchangeable hands and tools, so she can hold different things," says Swallow. "I like to think that's such a badass answer to Barbie, with her interchangeable high-heel shoes!"

▶ been continuously blessed with opportunities that have been really fun, and a lot of bizarre opportunities that have also always been fun for me as well. Doors kept opening so I kept walking through them!"

Those doors eventually led to *The Mandalorian*, which began inauspiciously for Swallow. "It was just a random audition, you know? I do a hundred of 'em. Some things are a really big deal, and some are just things that I don't really know what they are, and this was one of those things where I wasn't quite sure what it was.

"I knew it had *something* to do with *Star Wars*, but they were very mysterious about it and there was no one in the room working on the show itself, except for the casting director," she says. "I knew I was auditioning for a masked character who was the leader of a group of people in hiding, but the scenes that I read had no context whatsoever."

The casting associate during Swallow's audition was Jason B.

06

Stamey, who made a valuable suggestion that helped her form the character. "One of the things he suggested was that I do a take with a British accent, because they had mostly been seeing Brits in their fifties and sixties for the role. I'm not quite sure how I wound up in that room, but I'm sure glad I did!" Swallow laughs.

During production, Swallow was present when a special guest arrived on set.

05 Emily Swallow minus her Armorer helmet during a break in filming.

06 The Armorer (Swallow) showed her mettle against a squad of stormtroopers in Chapter 8.

"I was there the day that George Lucas came down to celebrate Jon Favreau's birthday," Swallow remembers with a smile. "I was actually on set when he started regaling us with all of these stories about making the original *Star Wars*, and it was mind-blowing to hear how, over 40 years ago and against all odds, he got that movie made even though a lot of people thought it was a ridiculous idea! And now, all these years later, here he is, watching people come together who still love his stories, and want to make new *Star Wars*. I mean, how must that feel to him?"

For Swallow, her *Star Wars* experience was over before audiences had even heard of the Armorer. "All of my work on the show was completed before there was an announcement of when it was coming out, so there was no pressure on set at all," Swallow exclaims. "No hype about it whatsoever. I could do my work the way I normally do, without any nervousness over working on something as big as *Star Wars*. After that, I just sat back and watched everyone go nuts over a show I'd already done. That was the coolest part." ☾

MEETING THE MERCS

Ever since Boba Fett first burst onto cinema screens, Mandalorian cosplayers have been a vibrant part of the *Star Wars* community, and they provided a cool moment for Swallow at a special screening of an episode of *The Mandalorian*.

"The entire audience was made up of Mandalorian Mercs. Just a sea of helmets!" Swallow recalls. "At the climax of the episode, when it looks like all hope is lost for Mando and Grogu, suddenly all the Mandalorians and I come out of hiding to protect them… and the Mercs let out this huge cheer. That felt so good—my people were happy!"

"WHEREVER
I GO, HE GOES."
THE MANDALORIAN

STAR WARS
THE
MANDALORIAN

Season Two Companion

We take an indepth look at *The Mandalorian*'s astonishing sophomore season.

WORDS: KRISTIN BAVER

ollowing its triumphant first run, *The Mandalorian* returned to Disney+ on October 30, 2020, with even greater visual and storytelling ambition than before.

Mando's mission to reunite the Child with his people evolved into a quest that took the pair to dangerous worlds, where the bounty hunter encountered several familiar figures from the *Star Wars* galaxy. Along the way, their bond became deeper, leading to an emotional season finale.

With a long wait until Season Three of *The Mandalorian* ahead of us, *Star Wars Insider* concludes our companion to the 16 chapters of this epic tale already available on Disney+.

CHAPTER 9
The Marshal

Directed and Written by Jon Favreau
First Airdate: October 30, 2020
Returning to Tatooine, the Mandalorian begins a search for others of his kind in the hopes of finding help to reunite the Child with his people.

The second season premiere began to connect the series more closely to the extended *Star Wars* galaxy, exploring creatures previously only hinted at in the original trilogy, like the krayt dragon, and introducing Timothy Olyphant as Cobb Vanth, an Outer Rim marshal who wore very recognizable Mandalorian armor that once belonged to Boba Fett. Vanth originally appeared in the book *Star Wars: Aftermath*, by Chuck Wendig.

In addition to Pedro Pascal's return as the bounty hunter known as the Mandalorian, the episode's cast list included John Leguizamo as Gor Koresh, Amy Sedaris as Peli Motto, and Temuera Morrison, making his first appearance as the unmasked Boba Fett.

TRIVIA

Numerous creatures in the second season owe their design roots to earlier *Star Wars* storytelling. In *Star Wars: A New Hope* (1977), the sand-scorched skeleton of a krayt dragon was all we saw of the mighty beast, half buried in the Tatooine desert. Concept designer Doug Chiang and his team were therefore able to reimagine the creature for *The Mandalorian* Chapter 9. The terrifying ice spiders from Chapter 10 were directly inspired by a piece of concept art created by Ralph McQuarrie for *Star Wars: The Empire Strikes Back* (1980).

CHAPTER 10
The Passenger

Directed by Peyton Reed
Written by Jon Favreau
First Airdate: November 6, 2020
A mysterious passenger with precious cargo joins the Mandalorian and the Child on their journey.

Chapter 10 took its lead from the genre-morphing fun of *Star Wars*, adding an infusion of horror thriller to the space-western, fantasy-saga vibe. After being forced to crash-land on a foreboding ice planet, the hatchling ice spiders that terrorized Mando and his associates had a birth cycle familiar to fans of Ridley Scott's science-fiction horror movie, *Alien* (1979).

TRIVIA
Having created its own library of quotable dialogue, *The Mandalorian* has referenced famous lines from other *Star Wars* stories. Chapter 10's, "This was not part of the deal," was a nod to Lando Calrissian's frustrations in *The Empire Strikes Back*. In Chapter 5, the Mandalorian's gruff, "She's no good to us dead," echoes Boba Fett's concerns from the same film.

In an episode largely devoid of unmasked human actors, Misty Rosas, the performer who embodied the ugnaught Kuiil in the first season, returned for an emotionally resonant turn as the character known only as "Frog Lady." To provide her voice, the prolific Dee Bradley Baker—known as the voice of every clone trooper in *Star Wars: The Clone Wars* (2008-2014, 2020)—lent the character his "frog speak" talents, while Richard Ayoade made a cameo as the voice of a now-dismantled droid Zero, last seen in Season One's Chapter 6, "The Prisoner." Comedy actor Paul Sun-Hyung Lee also made his debut as New Republic X-wing pilot Carson Teva.

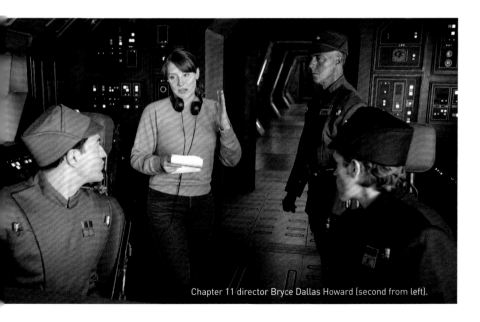

Chapter 11 director Bryce Dallas Howard (second from left).

CHAPTER 11
The Heiress

Directed by Bryce Dallas Howard
Written by Jon Favreau
First Airdate: November 13, 2020
The Mandalorian delivers his passenger to Trask where he finds trouble on the tumultuous seas and unexpected allies.

The trio of Mandalorians we met on Trask were led by Bo-Katan Kryze, played for the first time in live-action by Katee Sackhoff. Sackhoff, who has spent her career playing tough but vulnerable characters, already knew the role well, having spent nearly a decade playing Kryze—first as the voice actor for the character in *The Clone Wars*, and later in *Star Wars Rebels* (2014-2018). "She just *is* Bo-Katan to me," executive producer Dave Filoni has said of Sackhoff. Newcomers Mercedes Varnado (as Koska Reeves) and Simon Kassianides (as Axe Woves) rounded out Kryze's crew of rogue warriors, while Titus Welliver guest-starred as their fearsome Imperial foe. Giancarlo Esposito's Moff Gideon made his presence felt via hologram.

CHAPTER 12
The Siege

Directed by Carl Weathers
Written by Jon Favreau
First Airdate: November 20, 2020
Back on Nevarro, the Mandalorian reconnects with old friends to help rid the world of the Empire once and for all.

In his directorial debut for the series, Carl Weathers pulled double duty in front of the camera, reprising his role as Greef Karga alongside Gina Carano as Cara Dune. To round out the Season One reunion, Horatio Sanz returned (free of the carbonite slab) as the Mythrol, while Omid Abtahi's Dr. Pershing made a reappearance.

The episode introduced us to a very different Nevarro than the one we left in Season One, turned around thanks to the efforts of Magistrate Karga and Marshal Dune. In place of desolate streets and cronies of the Empire, a bustling, colorful market took center stage, and Karga had even opened a school—where the Child discovered a taste for "blue macarons."

CHAPTER 13
The Jedi

Directed and Written by Dave Filoni
First Airdate: November 27, 2020
The Mandalorian tracks down former Jedi Ahsoka Tano on Corvus in his quest to return the Child to his kind.

The live-action debut of Ahsoka Tano, played by Rosario Dawson, could only have been helmed by Dave Filoni, who co-created the character alongside George Lucas for *The Clones Wars* in 2008. The young Togruta was one of the first characters Filoni sketched for the animated series. Introducing Ahsoka, a veteran of the Clone Wars with long experience in the ways of the Force, gave the showrunners an organic way in which to reveal the true name of the Child—Grogu.

Although Ahsoka's debut had long been rumored, Filoni was reluctant to introduce the beloved character into the series any sooner than Chapter 13. "I intentionally did not do anything with her in Season One, because I didn't want to mess it up," Filoni has said. "Rosario's done all the research. She knows the character, but now she has to become it in a way that's never happened before." Ahsoka's live-action introduction also meant makeup designer Brian Sipe had to find the right balance between the character's animated look and a physical, real-world interpretation.

Exquisitely inspired by the Samurai films of Akira Kurosawa, the episode featured a cameo by Michael Biehn as the mercenary Lang and special guest star Diana Lee Inosanto as the Magistrate of Calodan Morgan Elsbeth. The Magistrate's face-off with Tano was the first live-action *Star Wars* duel to take place between two female combatants.

TRIVIA
In Chapter 13, Ahsoka Tano grilled Magistrate Morgan Elsbeth for information on the whereabouts of Grand Admiral Thrawn. Introduced in author Timothy Zahn's *Heir to the Empire* trilogy of novels in 1991, the cunning, blue-skinned Chiss has enjoyed a long literary history, and became the main antagonist for the crew of the *Ghost* in *Star Wars Rebels*.

> ## "I LIKE FIRSTS. GOOD OR BAD, THEY'RE ALWAYS MEMORABLE."
> *Ahsoka Tano*

WHO IS AHSOKA TANO?

Once a promising young student of the Jedi Order, Ahsoka Tano survived the Clone Wars, fought the rise of the Empire, and lived to see the New Republic.

The 14-year-old Togruta served as Padawan to Jedi Knight Anakin Skywalker for much of the conflict between the Republic and the Separatists. She ultimately walked away from her master and the Jedi Order after being expelled under false accusations of bombing the sacred Jedi Temple on Coruscant. But Ahsoka continued to fight for what she believed in, exemplifying the best qualities of the Jedi even as she claimed to no longer be a part of their creed, and aided Bo-Katan Kryze and her people to unseat Maul during the Siege of Mandalore.

After Order 66 was given, Ahsoka and her friend Captain Rex were among a few scattered survivors who endured the rise of the Empire's despotic rule. Using the code name Fulcrum, Ahsoka was instrumental in helping fledgling rebel cells form a cohesive Rebel Alliance in the time leading up to the Galactic Civil War.

CHAPTER 14
The Tragedy

Directed by Robert Rodriguez / Written by Jon Favreau
First Airdate: December 4, 2020
The Mandalorian suffers tremendous losses when the Empire interrupts Grogu's pilgrimage to an ancient Jedi site.

Chapter 14 marked the official return of Boba Fett and Fennec Shand, played by Temuera Morrison and Ming-Na Wen respectively, and saw the first true location shoot for the series. For previous exterior scenes, the crew shot on a studio backlot set or within the LED confines of the Volume to place characters on a variety of planets, but to fulfill the scope required by the episode's action-packed fight sequences, the crew traveled to Simi Valley—about 40 miles outside Los Angeles—for a shoot that called for numerous stunts. Director Robert Rodriguez pre-visualized the action sequences (turning three pages of script into a nine-minute sequence on screen) in a homemade animatic filmed in his own backyard, using his sons in costume and a handful of *Star Wars* action figures as stand-ins.

Stunt coordinators incorporated elements of Morrison's traditional Māori background to give Fett a distinctive fighting style that relied on fluid movements and barbaric brute force. "I've been waiting to see this version of Boba Fett since I was a kid," Rodriguez has stated, approvingly.

TRIVIA

Temuera Morrison was the perfect choice to don Boba Fett's iconic armor. In *Star Wars: Attack of the Clones* (2002), Morrison played Jango Fett, the bounty hunter used as the template for the clone army. Fett's payment included one unaltered clone to raise as his son, and the Mandalorian's timeline allowed Morrison to embody both roles nearly 18 years apart.

Chapter 14 director Robert Rodriguez.

CHAPTER 15
The Believer

Directed and Written
by Rick Famuyiwa
First Airdate: December 11, 2020
The Mandalorian enlists the help of an old enemy to get behind Imperial lines.

"The Believer" was a pivotal episode that challenged Mando's beliefs and showed just how far he was prepared to go in order to protect the Child. The crucial scene in which the Mandalorian removed his helmet to access an Imperial databank was only the second time audiences saw Pascal's face in the series, and the first time in the story that another living being had seen it since Mando first put the helmet on. "It's very economical and subtle storytelling," Pascal has said of the scene, "About risking it all—the value system, the Creed, and everything—to save the Child."

The return of Bill Burr as Migs Mayfeld, recruited unwillingly into Mando's ragtag crew for the daring mission, saw an impressive performance from the comedian, who imbued the character with a sense of profound loss.

> # "HE IS STRONG WITH THE FORCE, BUT TALENT WITHOUT TRAINING IS NOTHING."
> *Luke Skywalker*

CHAPTER 16

The Rescue

The Mandalorian and his allies attempt to rescue the Child but find they need more than just blasters to finish the job.
Directed by Peyton Reed
Written by Jon Favreau
First Airdate: December 18, 2020

In the unforgettable season finale, Mark Hamill made a triumphant return to the *Star Wars* galaxy as Luke Skywalker, with R2-D2 at his side. The episode also benefitted from its all-star line-up of characters from previous episodes, with Katee Sackhoff, Ming-Na Wen, Mercedes Varnado, and Gina Carano leading an all-female takeover of the Imperial ship helmed by Moff Gideon, played once again by Giancarlo Esposito.

The episode and entire season culminated in one perfect moment where no words were necessary. Throughout both seasons, Pascal's physicality and gruff vocals had lent the Mandalorian an air of distance, of unapproachability, and his helmet was the physical embodiment of that persona. Its removal, allowing Grogu to see his true face for the first time and touch his cheek tenderly, was arguably among the most powerful moments of the entire *Star Wars* saga. ☻

TRIVIA

Chapter 16 included a special post-credits scene teasing a new Disney+ series, *The Book of Boba Fett*. Set in Jabba the Hutt's old throne room, Jon Favreau described the set as a, "Crack for crack recreation of Jabba's palace."

TRIVIA

In the post-credits scene, Matthew Wood reprised the role of Bib Fortuna that he'd first played in *Star Wars: The Phantom Menace* (1999). The gluttonous older Fortuna of *The Mandalorian* had obviously enjoyed the fruits of power since taking Jabba's throne, barely recognizable as the slender Twi'lek originally played by Michael Carter in *Star Wars: Return of Jedi* (1983). The character's staff was a deliberate callback to an accessory packaged with the original Kenner action figure of Fortuna, never before seen on screen.

TRIVIA

Bib Fortuna's grunted Huttese phrase "maclunkey," was a reference to Greedo's additional line of dialogue in the 4K restoration of *A New Hope*, which quickly became a cult favorite quote that spawned its own hashtag.

THE JOURNEY OF DIN DJARIN

Insider takes a lightspeed look at Din Djarin and Grogu's story so far...

WORDS: KRISTIN BAVER

When we first met Din Djarin in Season One of *The Mandalorian* (2019 -), we knew very little about the mysterious warrior. A successful bounty hunter who favored a blaster and a blunt way of speaking, Djarin took his assignments from Greef Karga, head of the local Bounty Hunters Guild, while secretly communing within a Mandalorian covert beneath the streets of Nevarro City. Torn between these two worlds, he was a strict adherent to both the Bounty Hunter Guild code and the Way of the Mandalore. Finding Grogu changed everything.

▶

01 Moff Gideon was obsessed with capturing Grogu. Concept art by Brian Matyas.

02 Din Djarin's ship, the *Razor Crest*.

03 Djarin found an ally in Peli Motto, a Tatooine mechanic who took a liking to Grogu.

04 Din Djarin delivered Grogu to the Client, the vile individual who had placed a high bounty on the child's head.

02

▶clearly saw something of himself in the green creature's wide eyes. As we learned in flashback glimpses, Din was also a survivor, dodging a super battle droid attack that killed his family thanks to a Mandalorian who whisked the young boy to safety and took him in. Although Djarin was resistant to his pull toward the foundling Grogu, his conscience got the better of him after the young one saved his life in an altercation with a massive mudhorn. In quick succession, Djarin risked everything to rescue the youngster from the Imperial-aligned Client, a sinister man who had paid handsomely for Din's skills and his silence, allowing the hunter to obtain a shiny new set of beskar armor.

After freeing Grogu from medical testing at the hands of Dr. Pershing and betraying the Bounty Hunters Guild, the pair left Nevarro in Djarin's ship, the *Razor Crest*, and went into hiding on the world of Sorgan. However, it wasn't long before other bounty hunters were on their trail.

On a brief stop-over on Tatooine, where Djarin was forced to make an emergency landing for ship repairs, the mercenary earned some credits helping to collect a bounty on Fennec Shand, and made friends with mechanic Peli Motto, who quickly became enamored with little Grogu,

04

INSIDER INTEL

Favreau's Pitch

The idea for *The Mandalorian* was, in part, an homage to the film *Lone Wolf and Cub* (1972) featuring a Ronin samurai wandering Japan with a small child by his side. Creator Jon Favreau first envisioned the character of the Mandalorian around 2012, when Disney acquired Lucasfilm. Among his ideas were "an intimate, character-driven narrative, disconnected from the larger wars of *Star Wars*, featuring a lone Mandalorian gunfighter redeemed by the child that he must protect," author Phil Szostak relates in *The Art of Star Wars: The Mandalorian Volume I*. This provided the opportunity to merge Western imagery and samurai film tropes with a uniquely *Star Wars* spin.

Djarin temporarily left the child in her care.

Desperate for work, Djarin made another stop to see his old friend Ran, and agreed to lead an infiltration team during a prison break aboard a New Republic ship. But it was a surprise plea from Karga himself, who Din had left for dead on Nevarro, that brought him and the young one back to where it all began in the hopes of clearing his name and taking out the Client.

To prepare for what was almost certainly a trap of some kind, Djarin put together a crew: Cara Dune, a former rebel shocktrooper and brawler with no love for the Empire or those who still followed its rules; Kuiil, a patient Ugnaught moisture farmer with a succinct way of ending conversations with the simple phrase, "I have spoken"; and IG-11, a reprogrammed assassin droid Djarin had once utterly flattened. In a ruse of their own, Din agreed to return to the Client's office in binders to gain entry and catch him off guard, with a decoy pram floating by his side and Grogu and Kuiil on their way back to the safety of the *Razor Crest*.

But things went sideways, fast. Moff Gideon arrived, flanked by his Imperial remnant soldiers, and scout troopers caught up with Kuiil and

snatched Grogu from his arms. Pinned down with nowhere to go, Djarin and his friends barely escaped into the sewers while the Nevarro public house was all-but destroyed by blaster fire. But the Mandalorian covert had also been wiped out, leaving only the Armorer, leader of the sect reining from her ritualistic forge, picking up the pieces of helmets and other gear left behind.

She declared Din and Grogu a clan of two, placing the foundling in Djarin's care until he could be returned to his people: the Jedi. She also gave Din his signet and a jetpack, an acknowledgement of his ascent among the ranks of the now-fallen covert and his status as a full Mandalorian warrior. After one last fight—with Djarin mastering his new jetpack to battle Gideon head-on, Mandalorian versus TIE fighter—the threat seemed to be neutralized. But Moff Gideon was not so easily bested.

05 The Armorer led a covert of Mandalorians beneath the streets of Nevarro.

06 An Ugnaught named Kuiil became a friend and ally to Din Djarin.

07 Din Djarin and Grogu aboard the *Razor Crest*. Concept art by Nick Gindraux.

06

07

"Although Djarin was resistant to his pull toward the foundling Grogu, his conscience got the better of him."

The Nomad

While *The Book of Boba Fett* would go on to fill in the gaps of what had transpired between the time Fett was accidentally plunged into the Sarlacc pit in *Star Wars: Return of the Jedi* (1983) and his arrival in Season Two of *The Mandalorian*, his nomadic Tusken robes took inspiration from a film classic. Production designer and Lucasfilm art department executive creative director Doug Chiang has said he modeled his idea of Boba's nomadic garb on Omar Sharif's costume in *Lawrence of Arabia* (1962).

THE QUEST

In Season Two, Din's journey took him on a quest to find Grogu's people as well as his own. The series was about to take a turn and reunite fans with some of their favorite characters from books, animation, and film, with several making the leap into live-action for the first time.

In the season premiere, Djarin visited Mos Pelgo where another Mandalorian had been spotted on Tatooine. Instead, he found Marshal Cobb Vanth wearing the recovered beskar armor of the notorious Boba Fett. Vanth challenged Din's beliefs—a lawman in Mandalorian fatigues who didn't subscribe to either the Bounty Hunter Guild code or the doctrine of Djarin's former covert—and after assisting the town in slaying a monstrous krayt dragon, Djarin traded his skills for the return of the precious armor.

In Mos Eisley, Peli Motto (Djarin's friend and occasional babysitter to Grogu), had found a source that could lead the duo to more Mandalorians. But there was a catch—this source was a frog-like alien with a clutch of unfertilized eggs who demanded safe transport to Trask before she would divulge her information, and without subjecting her offspring to the jarring effects of hyperspace.

Traveling at sublight speed, the *Razor Crest* attracted the attention of a couple of pilots of the New Republic who recognized Din's ship as the same rare model involved in that earlier prison break. Crash-landing in an effort to avoid them, Djarin had to contend with repairs and a terrifying horde of ice spiders before they could safely get back on track.

On a Quarren fishing vessel allegedly destined for the secret Mandalorian covert on Trask, Djarin and the child nearly fell prey to a trap, but were rescued by Lady Bo-Katan Kryze and her soldiers. But Din—raised as one of the Children of the Watch, with stringent rules about never removing his armor or showing his true face—didn't believe Bo-Katan, the heir to the throne of Mandalore, was truly Mandalorian after she removed her

09

"Din revealed his true intentions to none other than Ahsoka Tano, Anakin Skywalker's former Padawan."

11

helmet. However, after saving his skin for a secon time, the two came to an agreement, embarking on a mission to steal weaponry from an Imperial freighter in exchange for intel that could help lead Grogu back to the Jedi.

After a brief detour to Nevarro, Djarin and his charge headed to the scorched forests of Corvus where the bounty hunter took a job from Magistrate Morgan Elsbeth: Kill the Jedi plaguing her world and gain a coveted beskar spear. But among the trees, Din revealed his true intentions to none other than Ahsoka Tano, Anakin Skywalker's former Padawan. Communicating through the Force, Ahsoka conveyed Grogu's sad tale to his protector. Raised at the Jedi Temple on Coruscant during the Republic's reign, he was hidden when Emperor Palpatine rose to power, dismantling democracy in favor of his new Empire. A survivor of the Jedi Purge, Grogu lived out his days in hiding until he was rescued by Djarin. Ahsoka—a survivor who walked away from the Jedi before Order 66 was invoked— declined to take Grogu on as her own apprentice. But in exchange for Din's help ridding Corvus of Elsbeth's regime, she sent him to Tython, where an ancient seeing stone could help Grogu connect to other Jedi survivors through the Force.

RETURN OF A JEDI
Ironically, Tython also brought Din's past to

their door. Wearing the fatigues of a Tusken warrior, Boba Fett emerged with his accomplice Fennec Shand, whom Djarin had once left for dead on the sands of Tatooine. While negotiating for the return of his familial armor, the arrival of an Imperial transport forced Fett and Shand to join forces with Djarin in order to defend against their common enemy. In the fray, the *Razor Crest* was destroyed from above and Grogu was kidnapped by Moff Gideon's dark troopers.

With the help of the convict Migs Mayfeld and Marshal Cara Dune, the motley crew broke into an Imperial mining facility on Morak to access terminal readouts that would help them track down Gideon's ship. The mission challenged everything Djarin held dear. After years of never removing his helmet in the presence of another living creature, he showed his face in a room full of Imperial soldiers to complete the facial scan that would help him save Grogu. It was a pivotal moment in Djarin's journey, from lone wolf mercenary to caretaker and defender.

Once more, Djarin gathered together a crew of allies, this time intending to storm Gideon's light cruiser. Among them, Bo-Katan, Dune, Shand, and Koska Reeves pledged their assistance. For most, the mission was out of loyalty, but for Kryze it was personal. In the ▶

08 Djarin and Grogu found Ahsoka Tano on Corvus. Concept art by Brian Matyas.

09 Marshal Cobb Vanth used Boba Fett's armor to intimidate anyone that threatened Mos Pelgo.

10 The ice spiders attack! Concept art by Christian Alzmann.

11 Din Djarin wrested control of the Darksaber from Moff Gideon, much to the consternation of Bo-Katan Kryze.

12 Paz Vizsla challenged Din Djarin but failed to win the Darksaber in combat.

▶ course of the Galactic Civil War, Bo-Katan had
lost the Darksaber, and the weapon that had
marked the ruler of Mandalore for centuries was
now in Gideon's hands.

Din succeeded in beating Moff Gideon in
hand-to-hand combat, his beskar spear deflecting
the Darksaber with relative ease. He freed Grogu
and took his foe hostage. However, Gideon's
contingent of dark troopers was too much
for the small band of fighters to vanquish
on their own. Just when the odds seemed
dismal, a single X-wing arrived carrying a
new reason to hope.

The Jedi Luke Skywalker had heard
Grogu's call through the Force. With his green
lightsaber ignited, he made quick work of the
dark troopers. Then he and R2-D2 took Grogu
to be trained at Skywalker's temple on Ossus.

INSIDER INTEL

The Secret Jedi

Luke Skywalker's appearance in Season Two of *The Mandalorian* was so secret, showrunners commissioned faux concept art showing Grogu's savior was Kel Dor Jedi Plo Koon, a personal favorite of executive producer Dave Filoni. Only a handful of people were let in on the Jedi's true identity before the episode aired, including those on set that day with Mark Hamill. "You see your crew just staring at Mark and you realize that they're remembering what it meant to them," Filoni has said.

12

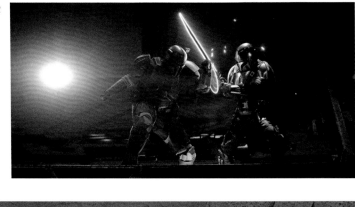

13

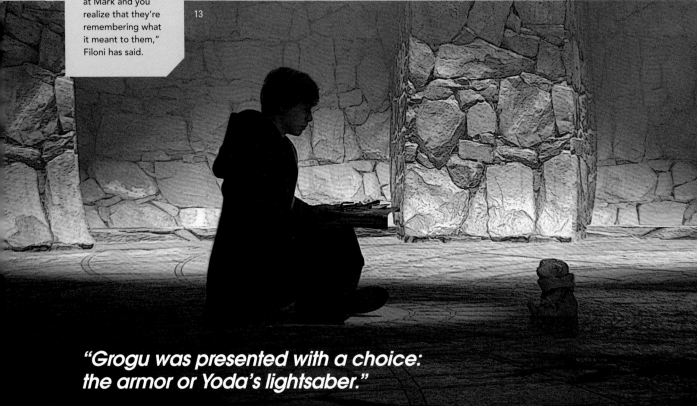

"Grogu was presented with a choice: the armor or Yoda's lightsaber."

14

16

What should have been a happy ending for Din and the child was bittersweet. Djarin had succeeded in locating other Mandalorian warriors and he had completed the nearly impossible task of locating a Jedi years after the Order's dissolution. But without the child to give him purpose, Djarin retreated back into his old habits.

LIFE IN EXILE

Din returned to what little remained of his covert, finding the Armorer and the hulking Paz Vizsla in hiding on the Glavis Ringworld. He went back to the work he understood, hunting down bounties in exchange for credits. But there was a distinct void in his life, a loss of purpose. Not even training with the Darksaber, a weapon foretold to make Djarin the ruler of his scattered people, could give him direction. And once it was revealed that Din had shown his face, revealing his identity in the presence of non-Mandalorians and breaking the creed, the Armorer ordered him exiled from his people.

Rudderless, Djarin returned to Tatooine where Peli Motto was prepping a replacement for his lost ship: a refurbished Naboo N-1 starfighter.

Meanwhile, on Ossus, Grogu was struggling

with his attachments to his former life under the tutelage of the Jedi Master Luke Skywalker. With the delivery of a gift from his adopted father—a tiny set of chainmail fashioned from the melted metal of the beskar spear—Grogu was presented with a choice: the armor or Yoda's lightsaber. Both gifts were valuable, but indicative of vastly different paths. Ultimately forsaking the restrictive Jedi doctrine, Grogu chose the armor and was reunited with Din Djarin amid a battle for justice on Tatooine that ended with Daimyo Boba Fett besting the criminal underworld that had profited from the sandy planet for generations.

With Din Djarin and Grogu together again, and the Darksaber still in the Mandalorian's hands, only time will tell where their next mission will take them.

13 Grogu's dilema. Concept art by Christian Alzmann.

14 A job offer awaited Din Djarin on Tatooine. Concept art by Christian Alzmann.

15 Din Djarin and Grogu reunited and bound for adventure.

BO-KATAN KRYZE:
LEADER IN WAITING

The story of the Mandalorian warrior's quest to rule her people.

WORDS: KRISTIN BAVER

Bo-Katan Kryze was a complex anti-hero and a conflicted warrior who was dedicated to her homeworld of Mandalore and its people, yet often at odds with those who sat on its throne. Even after the Empire allegedly turned her planet to glass, Bo-Katan remained steadfast in her mission to wield the Darksaber and retake her place as the rightful leader of Mandalore.

Star Wars Insider traces her story to discover how the heir of the Kryze line proves that morality and loyalty separates true heroes from savages and greedy outlaws.

Born on Mandalore, little is known of Bo-Katan's formative years, but she came to align herself with the world's ancient warrior culture. Wearing armor that was hundreds of years old, forged in battle, bathed in blood, and rich in history, the stoic Bo-Katan wore a helmet of white and blue, with the symbol of her elite fighters, the Nite Owls, emblazoned on the forehead.

In the time of the Clone Wars, her sister the Duchess Satine Kryze ruled their home with a pacifistic agenda, maintaining peace by remaining neutral in the conflict sweeping the galaxy. In stark contrast, Bo-Katan aligned with a terrorist cell known as Death Watch, a dedicated group of soldiers banished to the moon of Concordia and intent on restoring ▶

01 Bo-Katan Kryze was portrayed by Katee Sackhoff in *Star Wars: The Clone Wars*, *Star Wars Rebels*, and *The Mandalorian*.

01

02

"A HEADSTRONG REBEL WITH AN EGO TO MATCH HER DETERMINATION, THE YOUNG BO-KATAN SIMPLY DID NOT SEE HERSELF AS A LEADER."

02 The live-action version of Bo-Katan's costume as seen in *The Mandalorian* was a close match for its animated precursor.

03 Mandalorians Bo-Katan Kryze and Sabine Wren, in the *Rebels* episode "Heroes of Mandalore Part 2". ▶

Mandalore to a state that more closely resembled its cultural past. A headstrong rebel with an ego to match her determination, the young Bo-Katan simply did not see herself as a leader. "She's always reserved that for her sister [the Duchess Satine], for the diplomats and the politicians," Katee Sackhoff, who has played the character for more than a decade, has said. "She was the warrior."

For years, Bo-Katan worked closely with Death Watch leader Pre Vizsla, her signature double Westar 35 pistols and her Nite Owls in his service. As his trusted lieutenant, Bo-Katan was loyal to the cause above all else, including her own family. Bo-Katan was instrumental in the rescue of Maul and Savage Opress, and helping Vizsla and the two brothers to create the Shadow Collective, a united front that brought together underworld gangs like the Black Sun, the Pyke Syndicate, and the Hutt clan. Blinded by her beliefs and ambitions, Bo-Katan went along with a planned attack on Mandalore engineered to allow Death Watch to intercede and save the day, seemingly proving that her sister's form of governing had failed.

03

But the alliance with the former Sith Lord Maul resulted in a power-grab, and after Pre Vizsla betrayed the Zabrak, Maul decapitated him in his throne room. While most of the Mandalorian warriors in Death Watch pledged their allegiance to Maul, who now wielded the Darksaber and the right to rule according to ancient custom and tradition, the sight of an outsider controlling her world disgusted and horrified Bo-Katan. In a turning point for the warrior, Bo-Katan refused to yield and was forced to flee, as she and her Nite Owls were labelled traitors.

04 Bo-Katan teamed up with former Jedi Ahsoka Tano to liberate Mandalore from under Maul's rule.

A Reluctant Ruler

Mandalore's longstanding neutrality prevented the Republic from intervening overtly even as Maul and the crime syndicates he controlled seized the throne. But with the Battle of Mandalore raging and Kenobi rushing back to the Republic, Bo-Katan's survival instincts drove her and her allies in Clan Wren to forge an alliance with Ahsoka Tano, after Anakin Skywalker's former Padawan had walked away from the Jedi Order. Together, they mounted a siege to take back Mandalore and approached Kenobi and the Republic for reinforcements. With the help of half of the 501st Legion led by the newly promoted Commander Rex, Bo-Katan returned to fight for her people in the siege. But she quickly learned that she had played into Maul's hands, a trap of his making that would bring the Jedi within his grasp. And just as Prime Minister Almec was about to reveal the machinations in play—Maul's quest to bring Kenobi and Skywalker to Mandalore—Almec was assassinated before Bo-Katan's eyes by Gar Saxon, a Mandalorian loyal to Maul.

Clan Saxon and Clan Kryze remained at odds for years to come. Thanks to Ahsoka Tano, Maul was ultimately captured and ferried back to Coruscant for justice to be served and Bo-Katan and her faction regained control, apprehending Saxon and his loyal

followers. In the waning hours of the war, the Jedi named Bo-Katan as the regent to the Republic, but her service was short-lived. After Order 66 eliminated most Jedi and ended the Clone Wars, Bo-Katan found herself once more at odds with the newly installed government, refusing to obey the Emperor and his regime. She was betrayed by the Saxon clan who rose to power, forcing Bo-Katan into exile once more.

Bo-Katan's life during the long stretch of the Empire's prominence remains shrouded in mystery. But nearly 20 years later, just as the Galactic Civil War was on the cusp of breaking out, Mistress ►

THE DARKSABER

In the days long before the High Republic, the Mandalorian Tarre Vizsla was the first of his kind to join the Jedi Order, forging the Darksaber, a weapon which become the symbol of power held by the rightful ruler of Mandalore. At some point, the Jedi and the Mandalorians no longer saw eye to eye, yet the black-bladed saber remained essential to maintaining order and power on the planet for generations to come. A potent symbol of power, pride, and history, the Darksaber had to be won in combat to be carried by the rightful ruler of Mandalore.

04

05

THE SISTERS KRYZE

To paraphrase Ahsoka Tano, Duchess Satine Kryze and her sister Bo-Katan were nothing alike. One was a regal and benevolent ruler, longtime friend of the Jedi Obi-Wan Kenobi, dedicated to peaceful solutions even in a time of war. The other was hardened by battle, with a brusque manner of speaking that sounded like a growl, a no-nonsense survivor with no time for decorum and diplomacy. Bo-Katan never understood Satine's idealism; and Satine, in turn, never understood her sister's devotion to the perceived honor of the old ways.

It was clear that although the sisters' beliefs clashed, they were looking for the same outcome: a strong, independent Mandalore with a leader who would look after the needs of the people of their world. Polar opposites in almost every way, ultimately they were reunited by another's betrayal.

An organized attack from Maul and the various underworld crime syndicates made it appear that pacifistic rule had made Mandalore weak, an opening for Pre Vizsla and the Death Watch to succeed in returning Mandalore to its warrior ways in the name of defense for a fabricated attack. With the people on the side of Death Watch, Satine was removed from her throne and imprisoned, while those who stole her power used lies to cast her as the villain. Bo-Katan stood by as her sister was blamed for abandoning her post and her people, yet she could not continue to ally herself with Maul after he installed his puppet Prime Minister Almec and blamed Vizsla's murder on—of all people—the gentle Satine.

Instead of battling each other, the corruption of Bo-Katan's strict code of honor gave the sisters a common foe. Or, as Bo-Katan put it: "The enemy of my enemy is my friend." Bo-Katan twice risked her life to free her sister from prison, first so Satine could get an urgent message to Obi-Wan Kenobi before she was recaptured, and later acting as reinforcements for the Jedi as he infiltrated the prison to free the woman who loved him.

But the reunion of the House of Kryze was short-lived when Satine was brutally murdered by Maul to make Kenobi suffer. Despite her grief, Bo-Katan soldiered on. She infiltrated the prison system once more to help Kenobi escape captivity and prepared to take back her world in the name of Clan Kryze.

05 Bo-Katan came to the aid of Obi-Wan Kenobi after Maul brutally murdered her sister, Satine.

06 Her alliance with Maul proved to be an unwise move for Bo-Katan.

Bo-Katan the traitor still loomed large in the minds of her people, who believed her to be their true leader. Fighting alongside a rebel cell that included Mandalorian artist Sabine Wren, Bo-Katan was reunited with the Darksaber. However, initially, she refused to take up the mantle as the ruler of Mandalore. "I had my chance to rule and I failed," she told Wren. "I am not my sister. I am not the leader you seek."

But it wasn't long before Bo-Katan had a change of heart. "The Duchess," a brutal weapon of Wren's creation named for Satine and capable of targeting Mandalorian armor to turn the beskar that had protected generations of warriors to ash, proved that Bo-Katan could not outrun her destiny. If she refused to unite the clans of Mandalore, the Imperials would destroy them one by one, and she could not deny that Mandalorians were always strongest together.

Her world in ruins, a lifeless planet of smoking debris, Bo-Katan proved to be a leader whose cooler head prevailed even when the Empire threatened to annihilate all of her people, turning their sacred armor and all it stood for against the warrior race. Brought to her knees herself by "The Duchess," Lady Kryze survived to come back even stronger. As Wren prepared to turn the weapon against the Empire by targetting the armor of

06

"BO-KATAN'S DESTINY REMAINED TIED TO THE DARKSABER, WHICH WAS LAST SEEN IN DIN DJARIN'S RIGHTFUL OWNERSHIP AFTER HE DEFEATED GIDEON IN BATTLE."

Imperial stormtroopers, Bo-Katan appealed to her sense of honor and persuaded the young rebel to reconsider. Together they destroyed the abomination of a device.

Everything Bo-Katan did, she did for her people, her planet, and "For Mandalore." It was Bo-Katan, holding the Darksaber aloft and pledging her allegiance, who brought her people together. "I accept this sword for my sister, for my clan, and for all of Mandalore," she promised, finally uniting the disparate houses.

The New Republic
However, by the time the Empire fell and the New Republic was in

its formative years, Bo-Katan had lost custody of the weapon once more and it fell into the hands of Imperial Remnant Moff Gideon. Living in exile, Bo-Katan and a small contingent of fighters set up operations on the black market haven of Trask, stealing the needed supplies to take back Mandalore and protecting their own. On the watery moon they first met the bounty hunting Mandalorian Din Djarin and his tiny charge, Grogu, saving the pair from a boatload of nefarious Quarren who intended to kill Djarin and take his beskar armor.

A child of the Watch, a splinter sect that took the Death Watch's beliefs a step further to return to the most archaic Mandalorian customs including refusing to show one's face, Din Djarin and Bo-Katan were not easy allies. But by trading information—in the years after the Siege of Mandalore, Bo-Katan had maintained intel on Ahsoka Tano's whereabouts, a valuable piece of information on Djarin's quest to return the child to the Jedi—Bo-Katan was able to secure Djarin's help in claiming a cargo hold of weapons and an entire ship under the command of the Imperials still answering to Gideon.

07 Living in exile on Trask, Bo-Katan and her small group of warriors encountered another Mandalorian with his own mission.

08 Bo-Katan helped Din Djarin rescue his friend Grogu from the Imperial Remnant.

BEHIND THE SCENES

Bo-Katan Kryze is one of a handful of characters to transition from the world of animation to live-action in *Star Wars* storytelling, with a single actor portraying her in the recording booth and in front of the camera. Known for strong, complex characters, the actor Katee Sackhoff first voiced Bo-Katan in the 2012 episode of *Star Wars: The Clone Wars*, "A Friend in Need," working alongside future *The Mandalorian* collaborators Jon Favreau, who voiced Pre Vizsla, and director Dave Filoni.

Bo-Katan's destiny remained tied to the Darksaber, which was last seen in Din Djarin's rightful ownership after he defeated Gideon in battle. Although Djarin had tried to return the weapon to Bo-Katan, as Sabine Wren had before him, her adherence to honor precluded her from accepting his submission without a fair fight to claim the prize in victory. The destiny of Bo-Katan Kryze and her homeworld is yet to be written, but it seems clear that the leader in waiting is unlikely to relinquish her quest to resurrect Mandalore, with the Darksaber or without.

THE MAKING OF A MANDALORIAN

As Bo-Katan Kryze, Katee Sackhoff's *Star Wars* journey has taken her character from animated form in *Star Wars: The Clone Wars* to the live-action adventure of *Star Wars: The Mandalorian*. The actor spoke to *Insider* about how a part in *Robot Chicken* led her to the throne of Mandalore.

WORDS: JOHN KIRK

You know where you stand with Katee Sackhoff. Bold, direct, and possessed of an impish sense of humor, she's a galaxy away from the *Star Wars* character she has played since Bo-Katan Kryze first arrived in *Star Wars: The Clone Wars* (2008-2020). Sackhoff has made a name for herself playing such strong, warrior characters, most famously as ace pilot Kara "Starbuck" Thrace in the 2003 reboot of *Battlestar Galactica* (2003-2009), and as Niko Breckinridge in Netflix sci-fi series *Another Life* (2019-2021).

"I don't like to play uncomplicated women," Sackhoff smiles. "I like to walk a mile in someone else's shoes. In the case of Niko in *Another Life*, I wanted to live in the mindset of someone who knew that to save her child's life she had to leave her behind on Earth, knowing she would never come home again. One of the things I love about Bo-Katan Kryze is that I don't think being female has ever crossed her mind in relation to her capabilities or lack thereof. She's a warrior, yes. She's a woman, true. But Bo-Katan is an example of growth and redemption, forgiveness and atonement. She has tremendous

01 Bo-Katan Kryze (Sackhoff) in *The Mandalorian* Chapter 11 "The Heiress."

02 Katee Sackhoff as Bo-Katan Kryze.

"BO-KATAN IS AN EXAMPLE OF GROWTH AND REDEMPTION, FORGIVENESS AND ATONEMENT."

strengths but just as harsh weaknesses. She's real. She's flawed. She has a large ego, and it has cost her."

Career Goals

Sackhoff seems quite at home working primarily in the sci-fi and fantasy genres, and she credits her choice of roles to the influence of her father, who is a huge fan of both.

"My dad raised me on all things sci-fi," Sackhoff reveals. "I think I watched *Forbidden Planet* (1956) when I was four and I thought, 'This is awesome!' My father loves sci-fi and fantasy. He loves action. He's always been a movie guy and he usually had something playing on the weekends that caught my attention. He loves *Star Trek*, and it seemed like that was always on in our house. Honestly, he just loves anything in those genres. There's so much new content, especially now, that I feel like my dad is constantly calling me up, saying, 'Did you see such and such?' He's always just loved film and TV.

"The moment I had the chance to make choices in my career, I started going for things that I knew my dad would like to watch. When he saw me as Starbuck, I knew that role would not only change my career, but it would change the way people looked at me."

During the Vietnam War, Sackhoff's father, Dennis, served in the 9th Division until 1968. Has the actor drawn on his military experience for any of her roles?

03 Bo-Katan, voiced by Sackhoff, was a recurring character in *The Clone Wars*.

04 Kryze returned to the fray in *Star Wars Rebels*.

05 The menacing helmet markings of Bo-Katan.

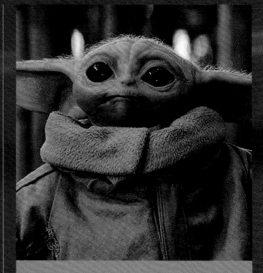

ASSET COLLECTOR

"I have as much Grogu stuff as anyone. I wanted to get one of those 'The Child' stickers for the back of my car. I have keychains, you name it. I'm obsessed," says Sackhoff, admitting her fascination with *The Mandalorian*'s breakout star knows no bounds. "My initial reaction to Grogu was close to that of meeting a dog. If a dog comes up to me, I have an immediate emotional connection with that animal, and I had the same thing with Grogu. He is real to me. It's the coolest thing ever, because during a scene he reacts to me, to what I'm saying."

"I didn't know my father as a soldier." Sackhoff says. "His time was served quite a bit before I was born. To me, he's just my dad. I personally don't focus on a character's career to inform their personality traits. I figure out what a character wants and what their vulnerabilities and strengths are. What makes them tick, so to speak. What motivates them. The fact that Bo-Katan and Starbuck are both in a form of military is not who they are, but what they do."

Playing Chicken

Sackhoff's chance to join the biggest galaxy of them all came through some voice work for a show famous for parodying *Star Wars* (among many other films and television series): the stop-motion animated comedy, *Robot Chicken* (2005 -).

Originally asked to play Starbuck alongside other members of the *Battlestar Galactica* cast in a sketch lampooning the show, Sackhoff was eventually given a recurring role in the series, playing a toy doll with the foulest, trashiest mouth any average eight-year-old couldn't possibly imagine.

"I DIDN'T NEED TO DO ANY RESEARCH! IT WAS *STAR WARS!*"

06 Bo-Katan's hopes for regaining the Darksaber were diminished in *The Mandalorian* Season Two finale.

"AS A KID, I'D WANTED TO GROW UP TO BE PRINCESS LEIA."

"That led directly to me becoming Bo-Katan," confirms Sackhoff. "*Robot Chicken*'s creators, Seth Green and Matt Senreich, were friends with Dave Filoni and one day he called them up to ask what I was like to work with. Thankfully, I'm not like the character I played on their show!" She laughs. "That's how I ended up working on *The Clone Wars.*"

As one might expect, having spent a lifetime watching science fiction and fantasy movies with her dad, Sackhoff was no stranger to the saga, so preparing for the role of Bo-Katan wasn't a strenuous task.

"I didn't need to do any research! It was *Star Wars!*" She grins. "I've told *everyone* who has ever represented me that if the *Star Wars* people ever called me, for *anything*, I would take it. I kid you not. If they'd told me to play the part of a rock and sit in the background, I would have taken it! When Dave

"One of the things I find so much fun about this industry is it's like a never-ending movie when I play a role, because I dream as my characters. I know that the moment I start dreaming as one of my characters, especially during the making of a show, that I've found out who the character is. I love that."

Among many highlights while filming *The Mandalorian* (2019 -), Sackhoff has most praise for her behind-the-scenes colleagues on the production.

"For me, what stood out most was the crew: the hardest working crew I've ever met," says Sackhoff. "They give so much to the series, and they do it because they love *Star Wars* and the show we've been making. I've made so many lifelong friends and am completely in awe of what they've created. Top to bottom, every department. Just outstanding." ☄

07 Concept art
   by Brian Matyas.

08 Din Djarin
   with Mandalorians
   Bo-Katan (Sackhoff),
   Axe Wolves (Simon
   Kassianides), and
   Koska Reeves
   (Mercedes Varnado).

09 A clash of creeds
   didn't stop Din
   Djarin (Pedro Pascal)
   and Bo-Katan Kryze
   (Sackhoff) from
   joining forces.

called me and asked me to voice the part of Bo-Katan, I jumped. There were no questions, I just said 'yes!'

"As a kid, I'd wanted to grow up to be Princess Leia. I'd also wanted to grow up to be Bruce Willis, but I really wanted to be in *Star Wars*. I loved that world! I loved what *Star Wars* was, so it blew my mind that the circumstances of my career had found me in that place!"

The transition to playing the character in live action was equally exciting.

"It was so crazy," admits Sackhoff. "I know my stuff, so I didn't need to work out the backstory for Bo-Katan. But when I looked at myself in the mirror on my first day in the suit, with the hair, it dawned on me that I hadn't asked myself how she moved, how her face moved, how her mouth moved! I needed to figure out how this woman warrior lived in her skin, and I realized Bo-Katan *doesn't* move! So, I had to throw out everything about Katee.

09

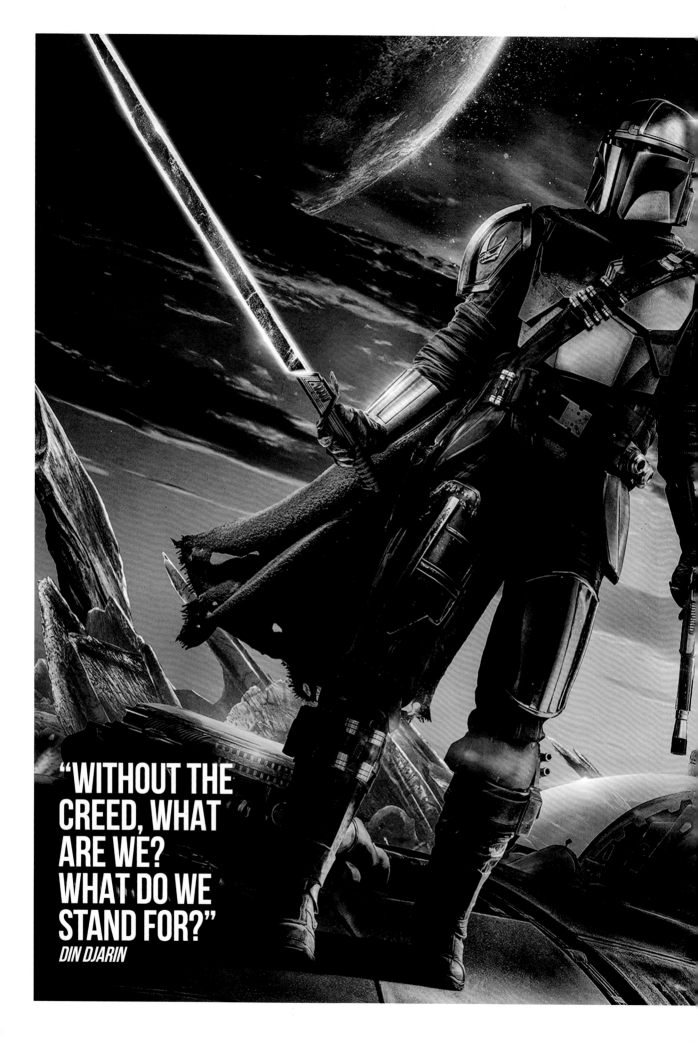

"WITHOUT THE
CREED, WHAT
ARE WE?
WHAT DO WE
STAND FOR?"
DIN DJARIN

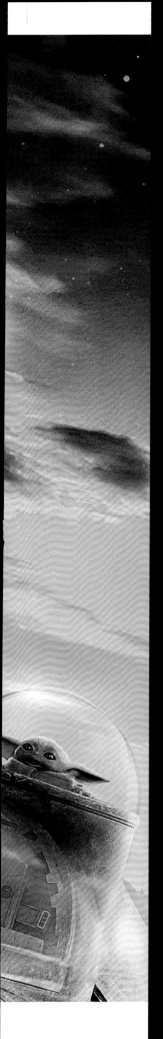

STAR WARS

THE

MANDALORIAN

Season Three Companion

The Mandalorian Season Three continued the adventures of Din Djarin and Grogu, reunited after some time apart and joined by Bo-Katan Kryze, in a series that explored their position within the Mandalorian creed and the history and destiny of the armored warriors. *Star Wars Insider* looks back at the unfolding story, with insights by creator Jon Favreau from a special press event in February 2023.

WORDS: JAY STOBIE

REPORTER: MARK NEWBOLD

More than two years after *The Mandalorian* Season Two concluded with the defeat of Moff Gideon, the transfer of the darksaber to Din Djarin, and Grogu's departure to be trained as a Jedi by Luke Skywalker, the series returned to Disney+ on March 1, 2023, taking the show in unexpected new directions. We would learn hidden depths about the Mandalorian creed, meet intriguing new villains, reunite with old friends, and finally discover the truth behind Gideon's secretive plans for a new Empire born of Mandalore and the Force.

"There's an inevitability to complexity developing over time," Jon Favreau, the creator, writer, and executive producer of *Star Wars: The Mandalorian*, revealed to *Insider* this past Februay. "That a show is going to go bigger and bigger, like the movies did. We're in new territory with Season Three, because we're dealing with lore that has developed from the choices that we have previously made."

Entering the third season there was a desire on the part of Favreau and his creative collaborators to be ever more ambitious in exploring *The Mandalorian's* central characters and themes, which meant a focus on Mandalore itself.

"We know what Mandalore looks like from *Star Wars: The Clone Wars*, and that there had been in-fighting there for centuries, so by having Din Djarin (from a creed that doesn't take its helmets off) meet Bo-Katan (who does), that allows us to bring those differences in Mandalorian culture into the center stage," Favreau explained. "That led us to the storylines you'll see in Season Three, which are a direct result of those tensions between the different factions."

The latest season culminated with the reunification of several of those Mandalorian clans, and that sense of coming together also relates to Favreau's approach to making *Star Wars* as a whole.

"People are invested in their expectations around our characters, and Dave Filoni and I have always been very cognizant of that," he said. "Whether you're a kid who's never seen *Star Wars* before, or you're somebody who has been following it all the way through, we want to make sure that everybody feels equally at home. We want to bring all *Star Wars* fans together and have something for everyone. Everybody is welcome."

Concept art by Christian Alzmann

CHAPTER 17
The Apostate

Directed by Rick Famuyiwa
Written by Jon Favreau
Premiered on March 1, 2023

In hiding on a desolate world, the Armorer is initiating a young member of her covert into the Creed when the ceremony is interrupted by an attack from a massive creature. Din Djarin arrives in his N-1 starfighter and dispatches the predator, before telling the Armorer of his intention to bathe in the Living Waters beneath the mines of Mandalore to gain redemption and rejoin the Creed.

Returning to Nevarro, Djarin helps High Magistrate Greef Karga fend off members of pirate king Gorian Shard's gang after they harass the local school. In reward, Karga offers the Mandalorian a job as his new marshal, but Djarin has a request of his own: rebuild IG-11 to help him explore the poisoned world of Mandalore.

When it is determined that the damaged droid needs a new memory circuit, Djarin leaves the planet to search for the part, but his ship is attacked near an asteroid field by a squadron of pirate fighters commanded

by Shard's henchman, Vane. Evading capture and destruction, Djarin and Grogu travel to Bo-Katan Kryze's castle on Kalevala to seek her help on Mandalore, but find her alone and without followers, who abandoned her as she did not possess the Darksaber. Convinced that Mandalore remains poisoned and barren, Kryze nevertheless informs Djarin that he will find the Living Waters beneath the ruins of its capital city's civic center.

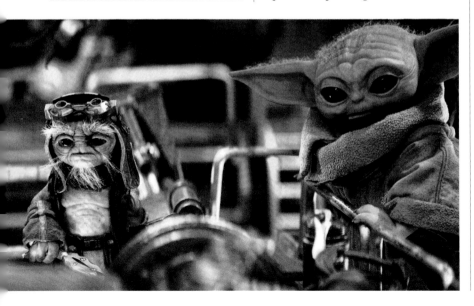

CHAPTER 18

The Mines of Mandalore

Directed by Rachel Morrison
Written by Jon Favreau
Premiered on March 8, 2023

Din Djarin and Grogu arrive on Tatooine during the Boonta Eve celebrations. Unable to secure an IG memory circuit, Djarin purchases Peli Motto's astromech, R5-D4, to assist him during his quest.

Concept art by Christian Alzmann

Passing through Mandalore's turbulent atmosphere, Djarin discovers that the planet's magnetic field was damaged by Imperial fusion bombs deployed during the Purge, preventing communications from the world reaching the rest of the galaxy. As Djarin and R5-D4 explore caves beneath the planet's crystallized surface, they are attacked by feral creatures. Scans also indicate the atmosphere is breathable—it seems Mandalore is less of a dead world than popular legend describes.

With Grogu joining the expedition party, the trio moves deeper underground in search of the mines, but Djarin stumbles into trap, set by a being who prowls the caverns inside a mechanical body. Held captive and disarmed, the weakened bounty hunter tells Grogu to find Bo-Katan and bring help, so the foundling races to Kalevala with R5-D4

at the controls of the N-1. Despite some misgivings, Kryze agrees to aid Djarin, and the trio flies to Mandalore aboard her *Kom'rk*-class fighter transport. Guided through the catacombs by Grogu, Bo-Katan uses the Darksaber to slay the mechanical jailer.

Kryze leads Din Djarin to the location of the Living Waters, into which he walks while reciting the Creed. However, Djarin is unaware of deep cracks in the crust beneath the surface and plummets into the hidden depths. Kryze dives in and rescues him but witnesses something unexpected and totally impossible as she drags him back to the surface—the unmistakable form of a living Mythosaur.

CHAPTER 19

The Convert

Directed by Lee Isaac Chung
Written by Noah Kloor & Jon Favreau
Premiered on March 15, 2023

A Mandalorian once again, Din Djarin collects a sample of the Living Waters to prove his redemption to the Armorer. Upon their return to Kalevala to retrieve Djarin's N-1 starfighter, Kryze's ship is attacked by TIE interceptors and are unable to stop a squadron of TIE bombers from destroying Kryze's castle. When Imperial reinforcements appear, the Mandalorians elect to make their escape.

Concept art by Christian Alzmann

On Coruscant, Doctor Pershing delivers a speech to New Republic dignitaries. Rehabilitated through the Amnesty Program, Pershing hopes to put his cloning research to good use in order to help others. Now working as a clerk, Pershing is frustrated by restrictions that stop him from utilizing his previous research for the benefit of the New Republic. Returning to his accommodation block, Pershing spends time with other former Imperials, including Amnesty Officer G68, who had served alongside him on Moff Gideon's cruiser.

G68 reveals her real name is Elia Kane, and suggests he finds a way of continuing his work unofficially. Pershing joins Kane on a trip to a disposal yard where Imperial Star Destroyers are being decommissioned. She has promised he will find suitable facilities there, but this was a ruse. Kane has betrayed him to the authorities. In custody, Pershing is placed in a mind flayer to undergo non-invasive rehabilitation, but when

the New Republic operatives aren't looking, Kane turns the equipment up to its maximum setting, submitting Pershing to an excruciatingly high level of exposure.

Meanwhile, Din Djarin and Bo-Katan Kryze return to the covert, where Djarin insists that the notion of Mandalore being cursed was a lie to keep them in exile. The Armorer tests the sample Djarin brought with him, confirming it was indeed sourced from the Living Waters. Since both Djarin and Kryze had kept their helmets on since being in the Waters, the Armorer declares that both were redeemed and now part of the Creed.

Concept art by Brett Northcutt

INSIDER INTEL: EASTER EGGS

The Mandalorian is a goldmine of *Star Wars* callbacks, but how are they worked into the show?

"It's very informal," Jon Favreau told *Insider* during the February press event. "We sit in a room with a board up on the wall, and we'll start to make notes about where things are going. Often, I'll write a scene and send it off to Dave [Filoni], and he'll say, 'This is interesting, but it wouldn't be that kind of ship!' He has a such a good working knowledge of everything *Star Wars*, so he'll suggest a ship from a game that was never in a movie that would be a good one to use. Or we'll talk to Pablo Hidalgo, or Doug Chiang, or John Knoll, or Hal Hickel. Everybody on the show is there because we love *Star Wars*, and everybody is an expert in a different era. I've used stuff like the Amban rifle from the 1978 [*Star Wars*] *Holiday Special*, and the camtono from *The Empire Strikes Back*. Things that we think will add a little bit more dimension."

CHAPTER 20

The Foundling

Directed by Carl Weathers
Written by Jon Favreau & Dave Filoni
Premiered on March 22, 2023

As the Mandalorians train at their hidden covert, Din Djarin puts Grogu forward to challenge another foundling. Initially hesitant, Grogu harnesses the Force to vanquish a Mandalorian boy in a darts competition. Suddenly a large raptor plunges from the sky and scoops up Grogu's opponent—Paz Vizsla's son, Ragnar. Djarin and Vizsla give chase, but their jetpacks soon run out of fuel. Bo-Katan Kryze, however, continues the pursuit in her Gauntlet, tracking the creature to its lair.

A small hunting party is convened to rescue the boy, intending to scale the peak where the creature's nest is located. Grogu remains behind with the Armorer, listening as she explains the importance of the forge to Mandalorian culture. As she talks, he remembers clone troopers attacking the Jedi Temple decades earlier, and the part Jedi Master Kelleran Beq played in aiding his escape from Coruscant. The Armorer gifts Grogu with a new piece of armor: a rondel depicting his mudhorn signet.

Led by Bo-Katan, the Mandalorian hunting party climbs the face of the cliff. The raptor lands at its nest, regurgitating Ragnar as food for its three hungry hatchlings. The creature flees when the Mandalorians attack, clutching Ragnar in its claws, but Djarin rescues the boy as the raptor plummets to its death in the waters below.

Triumphant, the group return to the covert and present the raptor's hatchlings to the Armorer as new foundlings. The Armorer prepares a replacement pauldron for Bo-Katan's damaged armor, and Kryze chooses to display signets of both the Nite Owls and the Mythosaur, creating a further tie with the Creed. She also confides in the Armorer of her experience with the Mythosaur beneath the Living Waters, but the Armorer chooses to see it as a noble vision.

Concept art by Christian Alzmann

CHAPTER 21
The Pirate

Directed by Peter Ramsey
Written by Jon Favreau
Premiered on March 29, 2023

Angered by the deaths of his pirates at the hand of Greef Karga, Gorian Shard arrives in his corsair above Nevarro's capital, intent on revenge. The ship opens fire on the settlement, prompting Karga to order an evacuation. Desperate for help, he contacts Captain Carson Teva of the New Republic, who promises to get the message to his superiors on Coruscant.

Teva meets with Colonel Tuttle in his office, where Amnesty Officer G68 happens to be working. Although empathetic, Tuttle says he does not have the resources to intercede. G68 also highlights the fact that Nevarro is not a member planet, further reducing the chances of New Republic assistance. Disgruntled, Teva tracks a signal from his old friend R5-D4 to the Mandalorian covert and informs Din Djarin of Karga's predicament.

Djarin petitions the covert for an intervention and Paz Vizsla stands by him, turning the vote in his favor. The Mandalorians head for Nevarro aboard Bo-Katan Kryze's ship, and while Din Djarin distracts the pirate's snubfighters in his N-1 starfighter, the remaining Mandalorians drop into the city, engaging in fierce combat with Shard's troops. After Djarin and Kryze deal fatal blows to the Pirate King's vessel in a blazing air battle, the Mandalorians liberate the city.

Karga welcomes Nevarro's saviors, bestowing them with land so they can call the planet their home.

The Armorer summons Bo-Katan to their old covert's forge and insists that she remove her helmet. Having interpreted Kryze's encounter with the Mythosaur as a sign that Mandalore's next age was upon them, the Armorer tells Bo-Katan it is her wish that Kryze unites all clans so they can retake Mandalore.

Elsewhere, Captain Teva dicovers a derelict shuttle, the craft that was carrying Moff Gideon back to Coruscant, floating empty in space, with the former Imperial nowhere to be found. Pieces of beskar are found lodged in the interior, suggesting Mandalorian interference, but it is unclear who was responsible.

CHAPTER 22
Guns for Hire

Directed by Bryce Dallas Howard
Written by Jon Favreau
Premiered on April 5, 2023

Having commandeered Bo-Katan Kryze's Imperial cruiser, Axe Woves and his Mandalorian mercenaries have been undertaking lucrative jobs for various clients across the galaxy. Hoping to recruit Woves' group to join their mission to Mandalore, Din Djarin and Bo-Katan Kryze travel to the planet Plazir-15, where its elected leaders—Captain Bombardier and the Duchess—agree to allow them to meet with Axe's privateers, so long as they seek out and decommission a group of malfunctioning droids first.

After consulting with Commissioner Helgait and Ugnaught engineers, the duo inspect some reprogrammed B2-series super battle droids at the loading docks. Djarin provokes one of them into attacking him,

resulting in a chase through the city before they destroy the errant droid. A spark pad found in the mechanical's possession leads them to a droid bar, where the bartender explains that every malfunctioning droid had drank from the same batch of Nepenthé, a lubricant that delivered program refreshing sub-particles.

Their investigation reveals that Helgait, the head of security and a former Separatist, had purposely caused the malfunctions due to his dissatisfaction with Bombardier, an ex-Imperial. Djarin and Kryze apprehend Helgait, and Plazir-15's leaders express

Concept art by Aaron McBride

their appreciation by granting them an audience with Axe's encampment.

However, Woves denies Bo-Katan's claim on the fleet of starships, so she challenges her former comrade to physical combat. Kryze emerges victorious, but Woves expresses his disdain for her unwillingness to fight Djarin to wrest the Darksaber from him. Although Djarin offers to hand the weapon over to her, Kryze understands that possession of the Darkasaber would mean nothing if she accepted it as a gift, but Djarin points out that she had retrieved it from his mechanical captor on Mandalore. By defeating the enemy who had defeated him, Bo-Katan had rightfully earned possession of the Darksaber.

With the power of the ancient weapon now in Kryze's hands, Axe, Koska Reeves, and the Mandalorian mercenaries willingly join Bo-Katan's quest.

CHAPTER 23
The Spies

Directed by Rick Famuyiwa
Written by Jon Favreau & Dave Filoni
Premiered on April 12, 2023

On Coruscant, Elia Kane informs Moff Gideon that Bo-Katan Kryze is now collaborating with Din Djarin and his covert. Gideon initiates a holographic conference with the Shadow Council, a group that includes Captain Pellaeon, Commandant Brendol Hux, and other Imperial remnant warlords. The officials agree to provide Gideon with reinforcements against the emerging Mandalorian threat.

En route to Mandalore, Bo-Katan's fleet arrives at Nevarro, where Greef Karga introduces Din Djarin to IG-12, a vehicle designed for Grogu utilizing salvaged components from IG-11.

Members from both the Nite Owls and the Armorer's covert volunteer for a mission to establish a safe perimeter on Mandalore, and a recon party is deployed to scout their homeworld's surface. They soon encounter Mandalorian survivors, who are surprised to learn that Bo-Katan had tried, and failed, to save her people by surrendering to Gideon during the Great Purge.

Din Djarin professes his allegiance to Bo-Katan, and the survivors guide them to the Great Forge, dealing with infighting among the tribes and a dangerous predator along the way. When the Mandalorians are ambushed by Imperial troopers clad in beskar armor, Axe Woves flies off to secure reinforcements from the fleet in orbit above the planet. An Imperial retreat proves to be a ruse, as it leads the Mandalorians into a trap.

Wearing unique dark trooper armor forged from beskar alloy, Gideon captures Djarin and announces his intention to use the base on Mandalore to build an army that he will lead to bring order to the galaxy. Rather than accept defeat, Bo-Katan elects to regroup and fight back. Providing cover for his Mandalorian brethren so they can make their escape, Paz Vizsla valiantly fends off Gideon's troops but eventually succumbs to an overwhelming attack from a trio of Praetorian Guards.

INSIDER INTEL: THE DARKSABER

Despite being an integral plot device in both *Star Wars Rebels* and *The Mandalorian*, the idea of the Darksaber only came about when a script for *The Clone Wars* needed a quick fix.

"Dave told me that there was a scene where a vibroblade was being used to parry a lightsaber, and George Lucas said, 'No, you can't do that!'" Favreau recalled at the press event. "That might seem like an arbitrary change, but George knew! He's got a good instinct. And now the Darksaber has become such an interesting, iconic thing. It's the foundation of what's happening in this whole series."

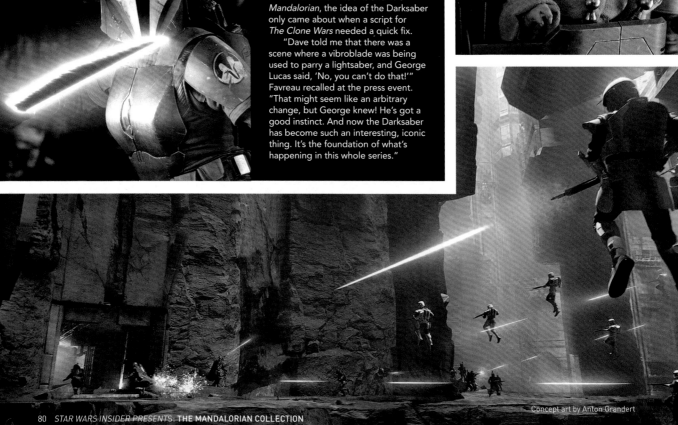

Concept art by Anton Grandert

CHAPTER 24
The Return

Directed by Rick Famuyiwa
Written by Jon Favreau
Premiered on April 19, 2023

In a bid to evade Moff Gideon's clutches, Bo-Katan Kryze leads the Mandalorians through the Imperial base and transmits a warning for Axe Woves to convey to the fleet.

With assistance from Grogu, Din Djarin breaks free from his captors and commits himself to killing Gideon. As he searches for his enemy, Djarin finds a room filled with clones of the Moff and initiates a sequence that destroys them.

Meanwhile, TIE interceptors have engaged the Mandalorian fleet, and Axe uses the cruiser as a decoy while his fellow Mandalorian escape the onslaught in Gauntlet drop ships. The Armorer and her Mandalorian reinforcements join Bo-Katan to assault Gideon's base. Wielding the Darksaber, Kryze and her troops battle jetpack-equipped Imperials.

Furious over his clones' deaths, Gideon faces off with Din Djarin and reveals his plan to incorporate the Force into an army of his clones. Grogu distracts the Praetorian Guards supporting Gideon, and Bo-Katan intervenes when Grogu needs help from Djarin. She can only watch helplessly when Gideon crushes the legendary Darksaber during their fight.

Axe Woves sets the Imperial cruiser on a collision course with the base, and the resultant explosion consumes Gideon in a fireball. Grogu uses the Force to protect Djarin and Kryze from the blast.

With the battle won and Mandalore reclaimed, Din Djarin formally adopts Grogu, who becomes his Mandalorian apprentice, while the Armorer joins with Bo-Katan Kryze to reignite the Great Forge.

Djarin and Grogu return to Nevarro, where a quiet life awaits them on a plot of land gifted to them by Greef Karga.

Concept art by Christian Alzmann

MANDO MANIA

How the secret of Grogu helped the first live-action *Star Wars* series make the space-fantasy saga a cultural phenomenon yet again.

WORDS: KRISTIN BAVER

ntil November 12, 2019, no one knew that the tiny being who became colloquially known as "Baby Yoda" even existed—at least no one outside of the tight-knit and tight-lipped cast and crew of *The Mandalorian* (2019-present).

In this age of online spoiler scoopers spinning rumors, offhand comments, and blurry set photos into endless streams of digital discussion, it was no small feat that showrunner Jon Favreau managed to keep the enigmatic, $5 million practical puppet under wraps up until the moment it appeared on screen in the series pilot, on the day that Disney+ launched in the United States. Trailers had teased the gritty western-inspired world of *The Mandalorian*, but none of the marketing had remotely hinted at what (or whom) would fast become the headline-grabbing face of the series. However, the show's instant popularity and groundbreaking achievements undoubtedly extended far beyond any single character or pop-culture touchpoint. By crafting an intimate and fresh story that required no previous *Star Wars* knowledge or viewing to understand, *The Mandalorian* was able to reach beyond the traditional fanbase and draw in an audience new to the galaxy far, far away.

As the first *Star Wars* live-action series, the show proved that the planet-hopping tales of adventure that fans had loved on the silver screen for more than 40 years could translate to television beyond its already successful animated incarnations. Critical reviews were promising from the outset, after a selection of scenes from the first season were shown at a press screening in October of 2019.

The team of series creator Jon Favreau and fellow executive producer Dave Filoni, who had previously studied at the side of George Lucas while making *Star Wars: The Clone Wars* (2008-2014, 2020), were praised by fans and critics alike for so effectively bringing a previously unexplored era in *Star Wars* storytelling to life on screen. Ultimately, the cast and crew took home seven Emmy Awards for its first season, including accolades for the impressive score, stunt coordination, cinematography, production design, sound editing and mixing, and special visual effects, as well as a host of other awards and nominations, including an industry-leading 13 nominations from the Visual Effects Society in early 2021.

But if you were to ask the next person you see on the street about any of this, there is one guarantee: whether they're a *Star Wars* trivia champion, a card-carrying member of the *Star Wars* fan club, or one of those rare birds who knows *of* Lucas' space opera but has never actually sat down to *watch* it (unbelievably, there are such people!), none could escape knowledge of the cultural zeitgeist of "Baby Yoda."

Baby, I Love You

In a roundabout way, we have Lando Calrissian to thank for the surprise revelation of the pint-sized character on-screen in the pilot episode. Favreau and Donald Glover, who portrayed a younger version of the smooth-talking scoundrel in *Solo: A Star Wars Story* (2018), were working on the Disney remake of *The Lion King* (2019) as the director was developing his own *Star Wars* story. "We were talking about ▶

01

music and pop culture, and he was saying that what people really like now is to be surprised, because it doesn't happen that much," Favreau told *The Hollywood Reporter* just a few weeks after *The Mandalorian* premiered. "When Beyoncé did an album, she would just put it online and everybody would react to it. Just putting it out there spurred a conversation that would become more viral and bring more genuine attention than any marketing."

It's a strategy that had worked for *Star Wars* previously. Lucas famously omitted Jedi Master Yoda from publicity materials and official poster art for *Star Wars: The Empire Strikes Back* (1980) to preserve the surprise, telling just two people—Mark Hamill and the director Irvin Kershner—about the twist that would change our understanding of Darth Vader and Luke Skywalker's relationship forever. But in the age of the internet, with rampant social media and click-bait headlines, it's even more impressive that the people tasked with preserving the secret of the Child persevered right up until the moment played out

onscreen. And the genius of *The Mandalorian*, beyond this best-kept secret, was often in the unknown. Favreau and Filoni's initial pitch banked on untold stories with all-new characters, exploring uncharted waters in a way that could succeed or fail without disrupting the stories that had come before. It was a safe bet for producers and consumers. If it was a hit, it could serve as an easy entry point for

01 Din Djarin (Pedro Pascal) and Grogu.

02 Jon Favreau with Amy Sedaris (Peli Motto) on the Hangar 3-5 set.

those with no previous *Star Wars* knowledge. If it failed, it didn't change the stories or characters fans already knew and loved.

To say it was a wild success is an understatement, with the Child at the forefront as the show's most recognizable breakout star. Perhaps it's no surprise that the diminutive creature captivated audiences; on set, the puppet had the same effect on cast and crew alike, winning over his first fans from unlikely corners

02

of the galaxy. Werner Herzog, the gruff actor behind the mysterious Client who paid handsomely to get his hands on the asset, famously chastised Favreau and Filoni when they prepared to reshoot a scene without the animatronic wunderkind, insurance in case they decided to completely replace the Child puppet with CG animation in post-production. "You are cowards," Filoni recalled Herzog telling him. "Leave it." The famed Germanic director later emerged as one of the biggest supporters of the character's creation. When he first laid eyes on the puppet, it brought him to tears. "It's heartbreakingly beautiful," he later told *GQ* magazine. "A phenomenal technological achievement but, beyond [that], it's heartbreaking." On set, Herzog was so committed to his craft and the presence of his co-star that while Deborah Chow was directing Herzog, he was directing the puppet as if it were a living, breathing being. "It was one of the weirdest and best things that happened with Werner," Chow recalled in an episode of the behind-the-scenes

documentary series *Disney Gallery: The Mandalorian*. "He was acting against the baby and he started directing the baby directly. I'm trying to direct Werner who's now directing the puppet. He would tell us we need to 'commit to the magic.'"

Herzog wasn't alone. Bryce Dallas Howard, who directed the Season One episode "Sanctuary," screamed when she first saw the Child; during her days on set she gave him a simple nickname: "Baby." Favreau shared a photo on Instagram from the day when Lucas himself paid a visit to set; in the image, the maker gazes down at the Grogu puppet as if he's cradling a child of his own. Even Giancarlo Esposito, who portrayed the nefarious Moff Gideon, couldn't repel cuteness of such magnitude. "Normally, I like babies... but in this case, I love this baby!" Esposito proclaimed at FAN EXPO Vancouver in February 2020. "I think it was a wise decision for them to have it take physical space, because that space allows all of us to be so

03 Mando met "the asset" for the first time in the series premiere.

04 Omid Abtani (Dr. Pershing) and Werner Herzog (the Client) filming a scene with Grogu.

05 Pedro Pascal as the Mandalorian.

wowed by its presence. I loved to be able to touch the baby. Oh my goodness, that baby's ears, when you touch its ears, it's so cool. It really feels real as well, so pretty amazing." And when the puppet was absent, on the days that Pascal entered the recording booth to capture audio for his character, the actor clutched a pillow in place of his pint-sized pal. The presence of the Child was essential at every turn.

Be My Baby

Once the world discovered the Child, there was a pop-culture explosion like no other. Fans wrote songs about him, and were hugely protective of the character. "Like everyone else with a pulse (including bounty hunter Mando), we immediately fell in love with ▸

06

the bone broth-sipping, frog-eating and cooing little creature," Tierney Bricker wrote for *E Online*.

The secrecy surrounding the character extended to keeping licensing partners in the dark until the show's premiere, so the first merchandise was a simple print-to-order model of a piece of heartbreakingly cute concept art of the Child by Christian Alzmann. That image alone hinted at the DNA of what made the character an instant icon: chubby cheeks, wide eyes, and just the right amount of baby-like naivety to fire off the same biological impulse that has us cooing at real babies of all species, ready to fiercely protect them against any foe.

06 Chapter 13, "The Jedi" director Dave Filoni with Dianna Lee Inosanto (left) and Rosario Dawson (right).

07 Grogu made his presence felt in class in Chapter 12, "The Seige."

08 The appearance of Boba Fett's armor in Chapter 9, "The Marshall" was just a hint of things to come.

Pre-orders for poseable action figures, huggable plushies, and collectible bobbleheads were open by December of 2019, while the Child's antics had become fodder for internet memes and social media impressions. Within the first month, two million Tweets were fired off including the fan-christened moniker "Baby Yoda." Mid-season, around Thanksgiving 2019, timelines exploded with countless takes on a clip of the Child flipping switches inside the cockpit of the *Razor Crest*, an endlessly customizable video that could be synced to pretty much any soundtrack or pop song, each one a delightful spin on the moment that made it seem like the kid was just trying to find his favorite tune on his space dad's radio. It was a

moment that resonated because of its humanity, a relatable vignette set in another galaxy. Another meme of the Child sipping from a bowl of bone-broth became the perfect fusion of throwing shade while subtly paying homage to that other green-skinned, mug-sipping icon: Muppet legend Kermit the Frog. It was essentially a meme of a meme, a send up of the Kermit clip that lent an easy-to-swallow shorthand to the Mando update.

By December of 2019, the Child was being featured in *TIME* magazine, held aloft with bone broth mug in hand in a painted portrait with Disney's CEO Bob Iger. Iger admits that the minute he saw the first footage of the final moments in *The Mandalorian*'s first chapter, he experienced the same feeling he'd had years before when he was running ABC's prime-time television wing and first glimpsed a young Leonardo DiCaprio on *Growing Pains* (1985-1992). "As soon as those ears popped up from under the blanket, and the eyes, I knew," Iger told *TIME*.

Baby, Come Back

By the end of the first season, art was imitating life. Even the stoic

07

08

ANATOMY OF AN ICON

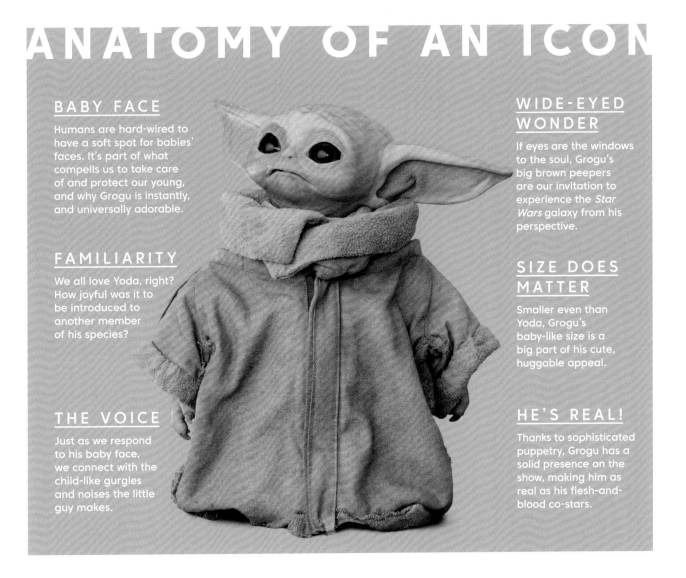

BABY FACE

Humans are hard-wired to have a soft spot for babies' faces. It's part of what compels us to take care of and protect our young, and why Grogu is instantly, and universally adorable.

FAMILIARITY

We all love Yoda, right? How joyful was it to be introduced to another member of his species?

THE VOICE

Just as we respond to his baby face, we connect with the child-like gurgles and noises the little guy makes.

WIDE-EYED WONDER

If eyes are the windows to the soul, Grogu's big brown peepers are our invitation to experience the *Star Wars* galaxy from his perspective.

SIZE DOES MATTER

Smaller even than Yoda, Grogu's baby-like size is a big part of his cute, huggable appeal.

HE'S REAL!

Thanks to sophisticated puppetry, Grogu has a solid presence on the show, making him as real as his flesh-and-blood co-stars.

assassin droid-turned-nanny, IG-11, had grown fond of the Child and was willing to sacrifice everything to help keep him safe. The titular Mandalorian had grown from a lone-wolf bounty hunter traversing the galaxy to the elder in a clan of two, repeating the same goodwill brought down by the Mandalorian warrior who had saved his own life when he was a child and welcomed him into the sect. And between Easter eggs—the casual mention of Cara Dune's homeworld of Alderaan, the first live-action depiction of the storied Darksaber, and the return to a post-Galactic Civil War-era Mos Eisley and the Tatooine cantina where our adventures first began—and the new characters, ships, and locations, *The Mandalorian* had become a cultural touchstone that managed the difficult task of delighting newcomers who had never before watched a *Star Wars* film, satisfying the most casual fans with its accessible story, and delivering the winks and nods that the most insatiable superfan couldn't get enough of.

With Season Two, which premiered at the end of 2020 on schedule despite the brutal global pandemic that forced most of its post-production to be completed with crew members scattered to their respective homes during lockdown, Mando's clan of two was set upon a new quest: to reunite the Child with his kind. Along the way, Favreau and Filoni took their hit-making formula and turned it on its head. Sure, the Child still maintained his adorable and cherubic presence in nearly every episode, hiding in his protective pram, or riding along in a low-slung satchel at Mando's hip. But the ▶

BY THE END OF THE FIRST SEASON, ART WAS IMITATING LIFE. EVEN THE STOIC ASSASSIN DROID-TURNED-NANNY, IG-11, HAD GROWN FOND OF THE CHILD.

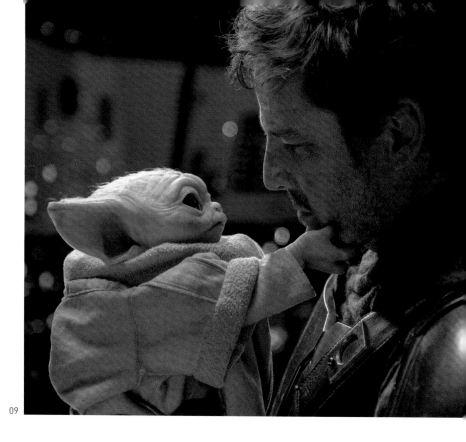

second half of Mando's journey was markedly different than his first leg. Buoyed by earlier successes and the deep galactic lore that preceded it, the showrunners resurrected Ming-Na Wen's Fennec Shand after her seeming demise in Season One, and pulled Cobb Vanth from the pages of a novel and into cinematic storytelling thanks to Timothy Olyphant. The season brought animated fan-favorites Ahsoka Tano and Bo-Katan Kryze into live action, the latter played by Katee Sackhoff who has voiced the Mandalorian royal for more than a decade. And Rosario Dawson's debut as Ahsoka fulfilled the destiny of Anakin Skywalker's former Padawan while clueing Mando and the audience in on a very important detail: the Child's name, Grogu. But perhaps most importantly, the series brought longtime fan-favorite bounty hunter Boba Fett back from the brink of death, scarred as he was from his time in the belly of the Sarlacc yet still as unstoppable as ever, and dared to deliver the ultimate connection to all that had come before. When you think about it, Mando's quest could only ever have ended one way. With so few Jedi left after Order 66, Grogu's plea through the Force summoned the hero who had helped redeem Darth Vader and defeat the Empire: Jedi Knight Luke

09

Skywalker himself.

In a season that had delivered so many surprises, the return of the Jedi had grown men and women in tears, thrust back to a more innocent time watching a young Luke battle the Empire in theaters and on their home VHS systems. "I'm not going to pretend that this episode's most dramatic surprise wasn't all the more incredible to me

09 Grogu and Din Djarin (Pedro Pascal) shared a heart-rending moment in the Season Two finale.

10 Mixing the old with the new is one of the many secrets of the series' success.

because I've been a *Star Wars* fan since 1977," Noel Murray wrote for the *New York Times*.

Like the arrival of the Child before him, even the actor Mark Hamill, who playes the legendary Jedi, marveled at the fact that his cameo appearance had remained a stunning surprise for fans at home. "The fact that we were able to keep my involvement a secret for over a year with no leaks is nothing less than a miracle," Hamill tweeted. "A real triumph for spoiler-haters everywhere!" That sentiment was driven further home by a shock post-credits scene revealing a surprise new Disney+ series coming in December 2021—*The Book of Boba Fett*—proving once again that perhaps *The Mandalorian*'s true secret of success is its delightful narrative balance of nods to the past, exciting new plots, and thrillingly unexpected reveals.

With numerous other *Star Wars* live-action series following in *The Mandalorian*'s successful footsteps, from an Ahsoka spin-off to the reunion of another storied Jedi and his former student in *Obi-Wan Kenobi*, it's clear that *Star Wars* episodic storytelling is here to stay, its successes no one-hit wonder, nor indelibly linked to the pinchable cheeks of Grogu. ☻

10

WHO? WHAT? WHY? WREN!

THERE'S NEVER BEEN A CHARACTER QUITE LIKE SABINE WREN. A CONFIDENT STREETWISE FREEDOM FIGHTER WHO LOVES ART JUST AS MUCH AS SHE LOATHES THE EMPIRE, SHE HAS CAPTURED THE IMAGINATIONS OF *STAR WARS REBELS'* FANS AROUND THE WORLD.

WORDS: TRICIA BARR

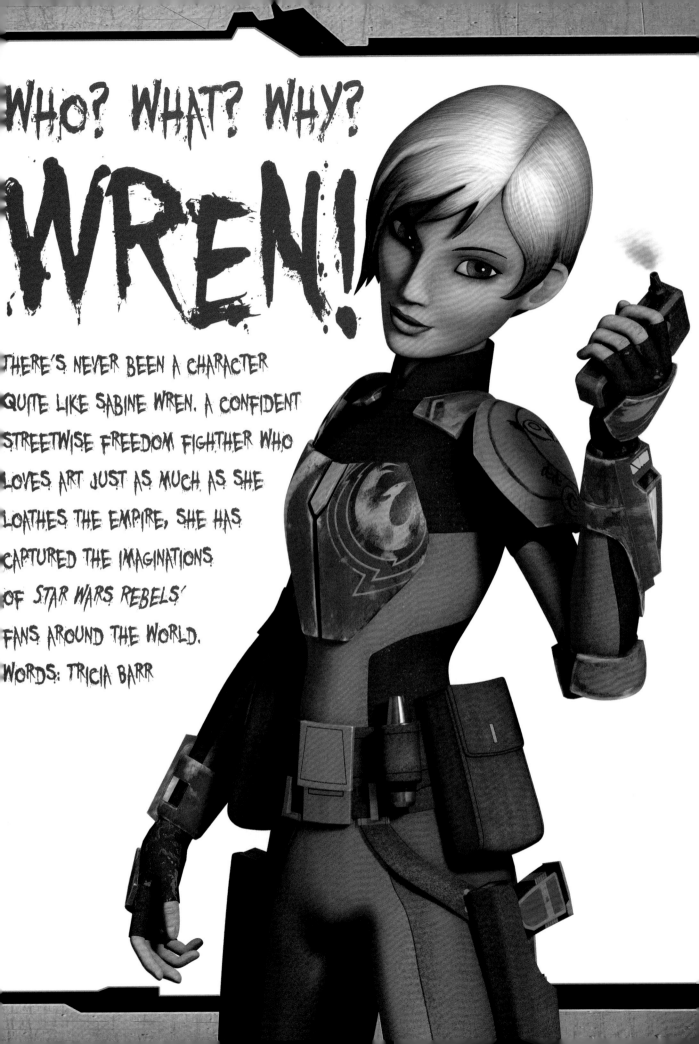

"FORGET THE EXPLOSION. LOOK AT THE COLOR."

—Sabine Wren, *Star Wars Rebels*, "Art Attack"

Speaking to the National Center for Women & Information Technology Summit early in 2016, *Star Wars Rebels* supervising director Dave Filoni talked about the lessons he had learned from the popularity of Ahsoka Tano in *Star Wars: The Clone Wars*.

"What we found was this amazing thing," he said. "When you create a strong, independent, intelligent character that shows no fear and can do amazing things, boys and girls like her. We've tried to create female characters who represent so many things, because we're trying to create a diverse range of characters. [But we've especially tried to create] female characters that are strong and independent. I want characters that are women of every race, every age and every description, doing interesting things and being dynamic."

When it comes to *Rebels*, there are plenty of female characters that match that description—not least Ahsoka herself. But one that has particularly captured fans' imagination is rebel and artist, Sabine Wren. When she took to the *Star Wars Show* Live stage at Celebration Europe, Sabine voice-artist Tyra Sircar was flanked by cosplayers from around the world—all dressed in her character's familiar Mandalorian armor. And as hints about Sabine's story in the third season of *Rebels* thrilled fans at that same event, there could be no doubt that her popularity is only set to grow.

WHO IS SABINE?

So what do we know so far about this enigmatic character, who will sooner express herself with an explosion than speak about her motivations? A member of the Clan Wren of House Vizsla, Sabine trained as a Mandalorian warrior from an early age. She attended the Imperial Academy on Mandalore before deserting to become a bounty hunter. She then joined a small band of rebels operating on Lothal under the leadership of Kanan Jarrus—a Jedi-in-hiding after the Imperial-sanctioned purge—and Hera Syndulla, captain of the *Ghost*. Over time, Sabine came to consider this group (which also includes Zeb Orrelios, the droid "Chopper," and newcomer Ezra Bridger) as something akin to family.

Yet despite her increasingly strong bond with the crew of the *Ghost*, Sabine has yet to tell them everything about her past, meaning that she remains something of a mystery, even after two years of travels and adventure. So what does Season Three have in store for Sabine, and what light will it throw on her warrior past?

SABINE UPGRADED

JETPACK

The jetpack that Sabine uses to flee Imperial Loyalist Mandalorians in the preview shown at Celebration Europe bears a close resemblance to the Z-6 jetpack worn by Boba Fett in *The Empire Strikes Back* and *Return of the Jedi*.

The only time we see Fett take to the air in the movies is when he travels between Jabba's barge and skiff in *Jedi*. But this scene highlights the limitations of such powerful gear, as it only takes a well-placed jab from the partially blind Han Solo to ignite the pack and send Fett careening into the sail barge before plummeting into the Sarlacc pit.

The jetpack made a triumphant return in *Attack of the Clones* when, pursued by Obi-Wan Kenobi, Jango Fett held his own in battle against the Jedi Knight. The jetpack allowed Jango to rocket away from the reach of Kenobi's lightsaber, and seemed unaffected by Kamino's relentless rain.

In *Star Wars: The Clone Wars* we learned much more about the Mandalorians, and saw in numerous action sequences that a skilled Mandalorian warrior equipped with a jetpack can equal a Force user in a fight.

DARKSABER

How Sabine finds herself in possession of the darksaber is a mystery to be revealed in the new season of *Star Wars Rebels*. What we do know about this ancient weapon, however, is that it was previously wielded by Pre Vizsla, the leader of the Death Watch faction in *Star Wars: The Clone Wars*.

Vizsla told Obi-Wan Kenobi in battle that the black-bladed weapon was stolen from the Jedi Temple by his ancestors during the fall of the Old Republic, with the sword handed down from generation to generation. Kenobi nearly defeated Vizsla, but he was compelled to retreat by the combined forces of Death Watch, which adhered to the ancient warrior ways of Mandalorian culture.

Later, Vizsla nearly killed Ahsoka Tano with the darksaber when she encountered the banished Death Watch on Carlac. After striking an alliance with Darth Maul and his Shadow Collective to overthrow the New Mandalorian government led by pacifist Satine Kryze, the Death Watch returned to Mandalore intent on seizing power.

However, Maul betrayed Vizsla, killed him, and took the darksaber as well as the throne of Mandalore. When Kenobi arrived in response to a distress call from Kryze, Maul killed her with the darksaber.

THIRD STRIKE!

During the *Star Wars Rebels* panel at Celebration Europe, Sircar hinted that figures from Sabine's past are set to appear in the new season, and there is a good chance that these could be (or could be connected to) the Imperial-loyal Mandalorians glimpsed in conflict with the *Ghost* crew during the teaser footage and trailer. She also mentioned that her character would come to the fore of the fight against the Empire, albeit somewhat reluctantly.

"Dave [Filoni] clued me into what was happening with more warning than in past seasons," the voice-actor teased the room full of fans back in July. "He used to say, 'Tomorrow, when we record, this is what's happening in Sabine's life!' This time, he's given me a better understanding of what's to come, which is awesome, because there is so much more to come for Sabine.

"I feel like I have a better understanding of who she is now, and I'm just as excited as the fans to see her experience new things and encounter people from her past... Sabine is being thrust into a leadership position, which she isn't exactly happy to assume, but there's a sort of pressure on her to get experienced. And then her backstory comes into play..."

Most of all, however, Sircar seemed excited about Sabine getting to wield some cool new tech. An intense clip shown at Celebration Europe and the following season trailer revealed that Sabine gets her hands on some iconic Mandolorian kit: a jetpack and Pre Vizsla's darksaber (see sidebar).

"She gets to hold the darksaber," Sircar exclaimed at the London event. "I had to steady myself because I was thinking, *What is happening? I have a darksaber! Why? What do I do with it?* It's all pretty exciting!"

STEM CELL

With all that to come, there can be no doubt that Dave Filoni and the *Rebels* team are paying more than just

lip service to the idea of strong, complex female characters in the *Star Wars* universe that reflect and inspire female achievement in the real world.

Sabine is just one of the members of the show's rebel cell who embodies the science, technology, engineering, and math skills that form the "STEM" framework that is so poorly represented among female characters in TV and film. And yet, she remains at the vanguard as educators reframe STEM as STEAM, to include a place in the acronym for art.

"I love that dichotomy that Sabine is this strong Mando warrior and yet draws beautiful paintings in her room," Sircar told *The Star Wars Show* recently. "Or, when she's blowing up the Empire, she leaves a little artistic signature."

How Sabine's art will feature in the new season remains to be seen, but it is worth noting that when Grand Admiral Thrawn is first glimpsed in the trailer, he is standing amid an array of artwork.

In Timothy Zahn's Thrawn novels, the villainous fan-favorite uses his enemies' art to better understand their motivations. Could Sabine's skills be her undoing? Surely not. But one thing is certain: we are guaranteed the complex character development that Dave Filoni has promised. Sabine's character arc is a work of art in itself. And long may it continue!

INTRODUCING BOBA FETT

THE *STAR WARS* HOLIDAY SPECIAL WAS NOTABLE FOR INTRODUCING A CHARACTER WHO WAS TO BECOME A KEY PLAYER IN THE *STAR WARS* SAGA, THE ENIGMATIC BOUNTY HUNTER, BOBA FETT. IN AN EXCLUSIVE LOOK BACK, THE HEAD OF NELVANA STUDIOS, THE COMPANY THAT CREATED THE SHORT CARTOON THAT INTRODUCED THE CHARACTER, DISCUSSES THE BIRTH OF A *STAR WARS* ICON.
WORDS: CHRISTOPHER GATES

"*Maybe I can help you. I am Boba Fett.*"

Gentle Giant's Boba Fett Holiday Special
Animated maquette, released in 2014.

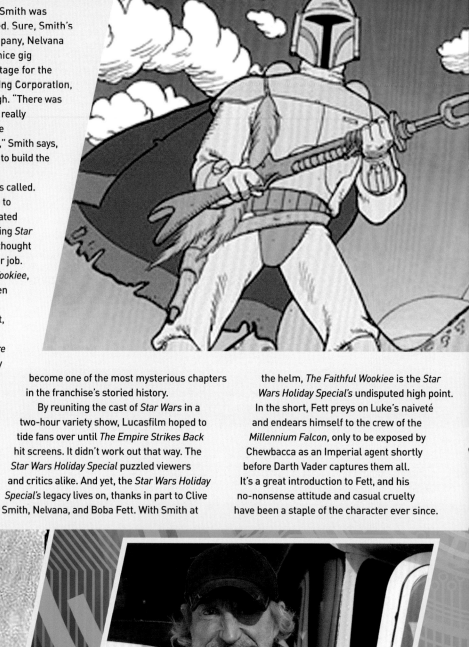

I n 1978, Clive Smith was getting worried. Sure, Smith's animation company, Nelvana Studios, had a nice gig producing stock footage for the Canadian Broadcasting Corporation, but that wasn't enough. "There was a point where we were really desperate to get into the entertainment business," Smith says, "Especially me. I wanted to build the animation studio."

And then, George Lucas called. Lucas needed someone to produce a ten-minute animated short for Lucasfilm's upcoming *Star Wars Holiday Special*, and he thought that Nelvana might be right for job. The short, titled *The Faithful Wookiee*, would feature a script co-written by Lucas himself, and would introduce audiences to Boba Fett, the villainous bounty hunter who hunts down Han Solo in *The Empire Strikes Back*. It was the opportunity that Smith had been waiting for, but it came with a catch: Smith only had two weeks to finish all of the storyboards and character designs, and he would have to travel to California to get George Lucas' approval in person. "It was pretty stressful," Smith says. Ultimately, the *Star Wars Holiday Special* would

become one of the most mysterious chapters in the franchise's storied history.

By reuniting the cast of *Star Wars* in a two-hour variety show, Lucasfilm hoped to tide fans over until *The Empire Strikes Back* hit screens. It didn't work out that way. The *Star Wars Holiday Special* puzzled viewers and critics alike. And yet, the *Star Wars Holiday Special*'s legacy lives on, thanks in part to Clive Smith, Nelvana, and Boba Fett. With Smith at

the helm, *The Faithful Wookiee* is the *Star Wars Holiday Special*'s undisputed high point. In the short, Fett preys on Luke's naiveté and endears himself to the crew of the *Millennium Falcon*, only to be exposed by Chewbacca as an Imperial agent shortly before Darth Vader captures them all. It's a great introduction to Fett, and his no-nonsense attitude and casual cruelty have been a staple of the character ever since.

Clive Smith.

SMITH ONLY HAD TWO WEEKS TO FINISH ALL OF THE STORYBOARDS AND CHARACTER DESIGNS.

BRINGING BOBA TO LIFE

It's a good script, of course, but it's Smith's animation that really brings *The Faithful Wookiee* to life.

In the early 1960's, Smith attended London's Ealing Art College, alongside future rock stars, Pete Townshend, Freddie Mercury, and The Rolling Stones' Ronnie Wood. There, Smith studied painting and "kinetic art", or sculpture with moving parts. "I liked to see things that were articulated," Smith says. "I loved the idea of things that moved with motions and hinges and stuff like that."

While at Ealing, Smith helped a classmate create an animated short and was immediately smitten with the art form. "It was the process that intrigued me, which was very manual, very physical, and very tactile," Smith says. After graduation, Smith parlayed his brief experience into a gig as an animator at Group 2 Studios, where he

worked on animated series like *The Lone Ranger* (1966-1969) and *The Beatles* (1965-1969). When Group 2 folded, Smith moved to Canada. In 1971, he joined forces with producers Michael Hirsh and Patrick Loubert to found Nelvana Studios.

Initially, Nelvana made ends meet by producing training films for industrial firms, short kids' movies, and "fillers," or videos intended to fill up airtime if scheduled programming ran short. The work didn't sit well with Smith. As a natural storyteller, he was eager to create something with a narrative. In 1977, Smith directed Nelvana's first animated feature, a half-hour CBS special called *A Cosmic Christmas*. The special caught George Lucas's attention, and he contacted Smith shortly thereafter about *The Faithful Wookiee*.

Smith might've had the experience, but getting *The Faithful Wookiee* ready in time wasn't easy. Even for experienced animators, two weeks isn't a lot of time to put together storyboards and character designs. The technology made it harder, too. "Remember, it was pre-digital," Smith says. "Today, storyboard artists do a panel, and they can do several different poses within that panel, and it takes very little effort to do it. We were using pencils and paper, and sticking things on the wall and moving things around."

Lucas sent Smith a script, and Smith got to work. Smith and another animator, Frank Nissen, locked themselves in a boardroom and cranked out hundreds of storyboards Meanwhile, Nelvana's designers plugged away, rendering the *Star Wars* universe into animation for the very first time. Turning characters like Han Solo, Luke Skywalker, and Princess Leia into cartoons wasn't too difficult; all the animators had to do was look at the original actors for inspiration.

With Boba Fett, a brand new character, it was different. "They sent us a black and white film of an actor in a mock-up of Boba Fett's suit," Smith remembers, but the design wasn't final, and the color scheme hadn't been locked down at that point. As the story goes, Boba Fett's costume was supposed to be sleek and streamlined, like a stormtrooper's. Smith disagreed. To play up Fett's warrior past, Nelvana made the bounty hunter's costume worn and battle-scarred. The rough-hewn nature of the outfit made its way into *The Empire Strikes Back*'s final Boba Fett costume, and has stuck with the character ever since. And remember, this was 1978. The *Star Wars* aesthetic was still in flux. Aside from the original movie, there wasn't much reference material available. Most licensed efforts of the time, including Alan Dean Foster's novel, *Splinter of the Mind's Eye,* and Marvel's *Star Wars* comic books, don't feel quite like the saga that we now know and love today.

Hasbro's Animated Debut Boba Fett action figure.

(SUDDENLY BOBA WHIRLS AROUND AND
FIRES AT THE CREATURE WHO HAS
BEEN BOTHERING HIM)

                    BOBA
        Force and threat are the only
        things that matter to these
        creatures.

                    LUKE
        I think the animal is only hungry.
(LUKE TAKES SOME FOOD FROM
HIS BACKPACK, AND FEEDS THE
CREATURE, WHO EATS IT HUNGRILY)
        This is all we have here, but you're
        welcome to it.

                    BOBA
        You are foolish to waste your kindness
        on a lower-form creature. None of
        them are worth going hungry for.

                    LUKE
        THEN I MUST HURRY & FIND MY FRIEND
        (There are more provisions on board
        the Millenium Falcon.)

                    BOBA
        You are of the Rebel Alliance, friend?

                    LUKE
        I am. Will you help me?

                    BOBA
        It will be easy for my creature to
        find the ship you seek. Follow me,
        friend.

2½

1

7

OUT?

10

14

A page of the script annotated by Smith, and featuring
Boba's fateful meeting with Luke Skywalker.

DRAWING INSPIRATION

In the absence of official reference material, Smith and Nissen took inspiration from the French comic book artist Moebius, who's famous for his psychedelic science-fiction stories. Smith remembers listening to Ennio Morricone's score for The Good, The Bad, and the Ugly as he drew, as well. To Smith, spaghetti westerns and Star Wars are a natural pairing. "There's that vastness of the desert, which in Star Wars is the vastness of space, and the details of the people within that environment, and how difficult that environment is, and how hard and coarse that is," Smith says.

Two weeks later, Smith packed his bags and lugged four carousels of slides from Toronto to northern California. He arrived at Lucasfilm headquarters early and lined the walls of an empty meeting room with storyboards. Soon, George Lucas and about forty other executives entered and took their seats. Smith began his presentation.

"I start talking, I start clicking through the slides, and telling the story, explaining what's going on in each shot, what the dialogue is, what the action is, what the effects are," Smith says. The Faithful Wookiee is only nine minutes long, but the presentation took Smith almost two hours—including one break, so that Smith could drink a glass of water. "Other than

THE FAITHFUL WOOKIEE IS ONLY NINE MINUTES LONG, BUT PRESENTING IT TO GEORGE LUCAS TOOK ALMOST TWO HOURS.

Cast

Anthony Daniels
as C-3PO

Carrie Fisher
as Princess Leia Organa

Harrison Ford
as Han Solo

Mark Hamill
as Luke Skywalker

James Earl Jones
as Darth Vader

Don Francks
as Boba Fett

Crew

George Lucas
(Story)

Ben Burtt
Sound designer/editor

Jenn de Joux
Video animation

Elizabeth Savel
Video animation

the perspiration falling and splashing on the floor from my forehead, you could hear a pin drop." Lucas spent the entire presentation fixated on the slide projector. Occasionally, Smith made jokes. Nobody laughed. "You get no feedback at all, you can only imagine that they hate you. What else can you imagine?" Smith says.

But the audience didn't hate it. When Smith finished his presentation, George Lucas clapped, and the rest of the audience joined him. Smith received a standing ovation.

From there, it was smooth sailing. Lucasfilm sent Nelvana the finished voice tracks (featuring Mark Hamill, Harrison Ford, and

the rest of the *Star Wars* cast), and Nelvana's animators brought the storyboards to life. Less than a year later, Boba Fett debuted on television screens around the United States, as part of the *Star Wars Holiday Special's* only official appearance.

Smith made his peace with the *Star Wars Holiday Special's* oddball reputation a long time ago, and is still happy with *The Faithful Wookiee*. "I was proud of the piece, and I know George [Lucas] was." Smith says. "I knew if we had not produced something we were proud of, I would've felt awful."

NELVANA ENJOYED A LONG, FRUITFUL RELATIONSHIP WITH LUCASFILM PRODUCING *STAR WARS: DROIDS* AND *EWOKS.*

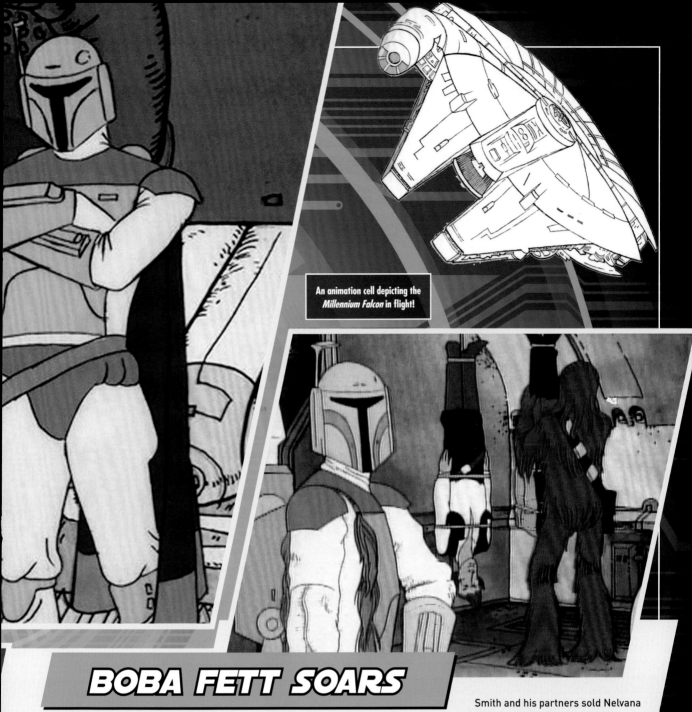

An animation cell depicting the *Millennium Falcon* in flight!

BOBA FETT SOARS

Boba Fett went on to become one of the most popular *Star Wars* characters of all time, and in recent years, action figures and statues based on Fett's appearance in *The Faithful Wookiee* have become popular collector's items. Meanwhile, Nelvana enjoyed a long, fruitful relationship with Lucasfilm (the studio produced both the *Star Wars: Droids* and the *Ewoks* animated series), and quickly grew into one of the biggest animation companies on the planet. Series like *Babar*, *The Magic School Bus*, *Strawberry Shortcake*, and *Eek! The Cat* all bear the Nelvana logo. Smith isn't a die-hard *Star Wars*

fan—when talking, he struggles to come up with key names and events from the series—and his relationship with the franchise is both more professional and more personal than most people's. When Smith talks about George Lucas, he describes a respected peer and an intense, insightful storyteller. He has similar feelings about the rest of the Lucasfilm staff. "George surrounds himself with people who are just as fantastic as he is," Smith says. "Not only were they brilliantly talented people, but they were also very approachable and very accessible."

Smith and his partners sold Nelvana in 2000, and Smith left the company in 2001. Since then, he's opened his own company, Musta Costa Fortune, and is hard at work on *The Rather Unusual Adventures of Ice Cream Girl and Mr. Licorice*, a full-length feature that will combine live-action with animation. Yet, while it's been almost forty years, Smith appreciates the gravity of his contribution to the *Star Wars* universe. "I feel really privileged to have witnessed and been submerged," he says, "for some period of time in that environment and that world."

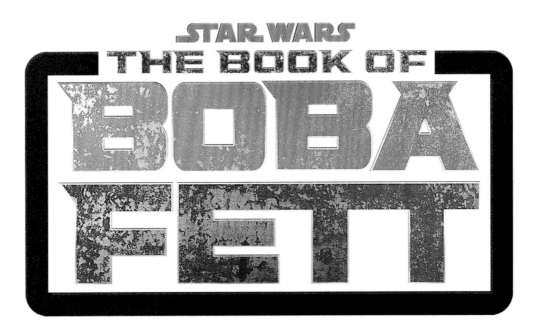

STAR WARS THE BOOK OF BOBA FETT

COMPANION

Long assumed dead, swallowed whole by the almighty Sarlacc in *Star Wars: Return of the Jedi*, it seemed like Boba Fett's fate was sealed—until the grizzled visage of the bounty hunter was briefly revealed in Season Two of *The Mandalorian*! *Star Wars Insider* revisits *The Book of Boba Fett*, the Disney+ series that documented the character's journey from mercenary to respected leader.

WORDS: AMY RATCLIFFE

The Book of Boba Fett (2021) followed the titular bounty hunter as he established himself as the daimyo of Tatooine, using flashbacks to fill the gaps between his ignominious fate in *Return of the Jedi* (1983) and unexpected resurgence in *The Mandalorian* (2019-present).

Now that some time has passed since the series aired, we can examine *The Book of Boba Fett* from a different perspective, rather than in the order events played out on screen. To best explore how Fett himself evolved over the course of the show, we'll look at each of its three main story arcs in turn, which,

in the grand tradition of *Star Wars* storytelling, can be seen as a trilogy of its own.

Recovering in a bacta tank from the devastating physical impact of spending an unspecified amount of time in the digestive tract of the Sarlacc, Fett experienced vivid dreams of his escape from certain death. Through these, we learned how he scrambled for survival, using every resource at his disposal to blast his way out of the beast and into the unforgiving glare of Tatooine's twin suns. The subsequent events told us not only how Fett survived and what happened next, but also showed us how those experiences fundamentally changed him. ▶

REBIRTH

Exhausted by the trauma of his ordeal with the Sarlacc, Fett lay unconscious in the desert. Utterly vulnerable to desert predators, Jawas stripped the beskar armor from his body in the night and left him for dead. Tusken Raiders discovered the dehydrated Boba Fett sometime later and took him captive. Their intentions for Fett, beyond using him as manual labor, were not entirely clear, but the legendary bounty hunter would surely have perished in the arid planet's scorching wastelands if they hadn't found him.

As Fett spent more time with the Tuskens, he observed them; he asked questions and tried to learn more. He saw a community, built on the strenuous nature of surviving on the planet they inhabited, with a respected hierarchy and strong emotional bonds. It was nothing like the life he himself had lived.

Boba Fett was born in a different era, during a war that consumed the galaxy. He lost his father at a young age, killed by a Jedi, and his desire for revenge drove the orphaned boy to survive. For a time, the ambitious youth found a family of sorts within a bounty hunter gang,

01 Badly injured, Fett had to fight his way out of the Sarlacc's belly.

02 Tusken Raiders captured Fett and used him to scavenge for black melons in the desert.

03 Fett led the Tuskens on a raid against a Pyke Syndicate spice shipment.

04 Saving a Tusken child from an attacking Tatooine sand beast gained Fett the respect of the tribe's leader. Concept art by Christian Alzmann.

but as he grew older, he worked alone. Like most individuals in his trade, Fett led a solitary existence, moving from one job to the next. Yet with the Tuskens, he began to recognize a place where he could belong, and he started cooperating instead of trying to escape.

01

02

03

04

His physical strength played a role; Fett helped procure black melons, a staple food in Tusken culture, and protected a Tusken child from a Tatooine sand beast. These acts earned Fett their respect. When Boba became aware of the Pyke Syndicate's spice operations on Tatooine and how the criminals were killing Tuskens at will, he helped the tribe take decisive action. The bounty hunter taught the Tuskens how to use outsider technology and equipment such as speeder bikes so they could stand on a more equal footing with their enemies. Any skepticism of the foreign vehicles and techniques was outweighed by the desire to defend their desert home from the Pykes and their illicit

trade. After Fett successfully stopped a Pyke repulsor train and demanded a toll for any further use of Tusken lands, the Tusken Raiders accepted him into their tribe. It was an honor he happily embraced, fully immersing himself in their traditions and way of life. At long last, he had found his place in the galaxy. He had found a family, a home.

The Pyke Syndicate had other ideas. Boba Fett showed his commitment to this new life by paying the local Pyke leader a visit in Mos Eisley. But even as he demanded they respect and pay the Tuskens for utilizing the land that had been theirs since the oceans of Tatooine dried, the Pykes were exacting a devastating revenge on the Tusken tribe, slaughtering them all and leaving evidence to shift the blame onto a local Nikto gang, the Kintan Striders. When Fett stumbled into the burning encampment, he found himself in a familiar territory—lost, alone, and angry.   ▶

05 Returning from Mos Eisley, Fett discovered his new tribe had been brutally wiped out.

06 Fett attacked the Kintan Striders, believing they were behind the slaughter of his Tusken tribe. Concept art by Ryan Church.

THE TREE

As part of his initiation into the Tusken Raider tribe, Boba Fett was gifted with an innocuous-looking lizard that the Tusken chief explained was a guide. The creature launched itself into Fett's nostril and induced a hallucinatory experience in which Boba saw aspects of his former life—the roiling seascape of Kamino, his armor, and the Sarlacc's stomach. The vision culminated in the limbs of a Tatooine wortwood tree wrapping themselves around the armored Fett. But what did it all mean?

A number of Indigenous Earth cultures participate in vision quests as rites of passage, sometimes focusing on younger members (usually male) as they attain adulthood, and sometimes for the purpose of gaining courage or seeking favor from the spirits. Trees are symbols of guidance, unity, and sacrifice in some cultures and religions, and the imagery was certainly apt for this turning point in Boba Fett's life. In *The Empire Strikes Back* (1980), Luke Skywalker had his own vision of Darth Vader while in the roots of a tree infused with the dark side on Dagobah. He would later learn that Vader was his father. Did the tree in Fett's vision imply that he was not alone but part of something bigger, or that his destiny could take many different paths? It is open to interpretation.

06

THE BATTLE FOR
MOS ESPA

08

09

08 Boba Fett and
Fennec Shand
combined forces
to recover Fett's
ship and take
out Bib Fortuna.

09 The Pyke's
duplicity over
their previous
deal didn't sit
well with Fett.
His only option
to defend the
people of Mos
Espa was to
go to war with
the Syndicate.

Boba Fett found a new place in the galaxy, and almost as quickly, he lost it after the Pykes coordinated the attack on the Tuskens. He went from joining a tribe to wandering Tatooine's desert alone, with only his bantha for company. The pair spent an unknown amount of time leading a nomadic life together. Fett seemingly scouted near Jabba's palace regularly, seeing if it was feasible for him to overcome the guards to take back his customized *Firespray-31*-class attack craft. He was unable to find a safe way in and felt too vulnerable without his armor. Beaten, lost, and once again on his own, Fett and his bantha led a quiet life in the sands until Fett spotted a fateful flare.

The light in the desert's sky led Boba and his steed to an unconcious woman who had been left for dead with a critical wound. Recognizing her as the master assassin Fennec Shand, Fett saw a potential ally. He took the injured assassin to a Mos Eisley mod parlor and paid the price for an artist known as the Modifier to work on Fennec. Using intricate cybernetics, he saved her from what should have been a lethal shot to the gut.

Boba explained his goal of exacting revenge upon Jabba for double-crossing him and how he needed Shand's assistance to accomplish it. Cynical of a bounty hunter changing their fate, Fennec agreed, somewhat reluctantly, to help Fett, as a

DIN DJARIN'S JOURNEY

12

When we last saw Din Djarin, the Mandalorian had set aside the Way to remove his helmet and look his foundling, Grogu, in the eyes before sending the child to follow his destiny with the Jedi Luke Skywalker. Trying to find his path back to his fellow Mandalorians and the Way after the incident on Nevarro, Djarin tracked his Mandalorian tribe

to their hideout. The Armorer related the Darksaber's history and the events of "The Night of a Thousand Tears," after which Djarin admitted he had not followed the Way. His tribe immediately shunned him.

Meanwhile, on the planet Ossus, Grogu similarly struggled with following his destiny. Luke trained the youth, but Grogu's

heart didn't seem to be in it. After Djarin left a gift for his friend, Luke gave the youngling a choice: reject it and continue training or accept Djarin's gift and leave. Grogu chose to depart and find Din Djarin, the being who had rescued him and taken care of him.

Though the galaxy presented both the Mandalorian and the

foundling with set paths, both chose to diverge; and in doing so, they came back together to help another who had made his own way: Boba Fett.

way to repay him for saving her life. After successfully extracting Fett's ship from Jabba's palace, which Bib Fortuna had taken over, Boba and Fennec formed an alliance. They took care of his loose ends, and Fennec supported Fett's goals of taking over Jabba's seat.

Boba was tired of the way other crime syndicates had been running their operations and weary of being at the mercy of employers whose idiocy was likely to get Fett, Fennec, and others like them killed. In becoming the new daimyo of Tatooine, Fett saw an opportunity to do better. He would be well positioned to take on the Pyke ▶

10 Cad Bane, an old foe of Fett's, was on the Pyke's payroll.

11 Cobb Vanth, Marshal of Freetown, was gunned down by Cad Bane after he confronted members of the Pyke Syndicate.

12 Grogu faced a difficult decision set by Jedi Master Luke Skywalker.

13 Din Djarin attempted to visit Grogu before returning to Tatooine to help Boba Fett.

EPISODE BY EPISODE

Chapter 1:
"Stranger in a Strange Land"

Directed by Robert Rodriguez
Written by Jon Favreau
Premiered: December 29, 2021

Boba Fett works with Fennec Shand to secure Jabba's empire and recalls his escape from the Sarlacc and his time with the Tusken Raiders who captured him.

Chapter 2:
"The Tribes of Tatooine"

Directed by Steph Green
Written by Jon Favreau
Premiered: January 5, 2022

Jabba's cousins send the Wookiee bounty hunter Krrsantan to kill Boba Fett and pave the way for them to lead on Tatooine. Fett's memories show the Pyke Syndicate's influence on the desert planet.

Chapter 3:
"The Streets of Mos Espa"

Directed by Robert Rodriguez
Written by Jon Favreau
Premiered: January 12, 2022

Boba Fett and the Twins learn the mayor of Mos Espa promised Jabba's territory to the Pyke Syndicate, a group Fett and the Tuskens had problems with in the past.

Chapter 4:
"The Gathering Storm"

Directed by Kevin Tancharoen
Written by Jon Favreau
Premiered: January 19, 2022

Boba Fett remembers discovering Fennec Shand dying in the desert and getting her help to take Jabba's throne. In the present, Fett calls a meeting with Mos Espa's crime bosses.

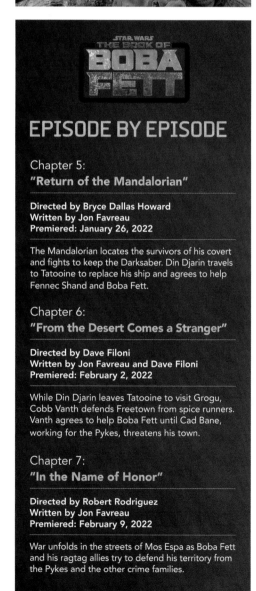

15 Allies from across Tatooine joined Fett in a final battle against the Pykes on the streets of Mos Espa.

16 Even the diminutive Grogu played his part in the battle, calming Fett's raging rancor.

Syndicate and to stop the spice trade from causing additional harm to the innocent citizens of the planet—innocents like his Tusken family. After working for a number of foolish and cruel beings around the galaxy, Boba knew he would approach his rule with less of an iron fist and more of an open hand. He didn't want to head a thoughtless crime syndicate that would oppress others. Boba Fett wanted those he worked with to have a say in their own destiny.

Based on the number of allies who came to Mos Espa to help Boba Fett make a stand against the Pykes and other crime families, Boba Fett's approach to being daimyo was successful.

CHANGED MAN

From a youth seeking revenge for his father's death to a hardened bounty hunter, Boba Fett's fierce reputation didn't include mercy. He ran a syndicate of bounty hunters from a young age, became a reliable hired-gun for Jabba the Hutt, and hunted down Luke Skywalker at the behest of Darth Vader. Fett didn't care who he worked for as long as he got paid. Yet after cheating certain death within the belly of the Sarlacc and finding a new place in the galaxy among the Tuskens of Tatooine, the bounty hunter was a changed man.

After getting back his precious armor, and removing Bib Fortuna from Jabba's throne, Fett seemed to look upon the galaxy differently.

Despite Fennec Shand's recommendations to be ruthless, Fett established a different approach as soon as he claimed the position of daimyo. He didn't want to rule

with fear. Instead, the former bounty hunter preferred to rule with respect and with a mind towards building a community. Boba Fett shed layers of hardness and coldness and showed mercy where Jabba would have thrown whatever the problem was into his rancor pit and moved on. Perhaps changed by his experiences in Tatooine's desert, Fett's magnanimous attitude led him to hire a group of modified humans, called the Mods, who were stealing water because the water-monger was overpricing it and exploiting those in need. Fett also kept Jabba's Gamorrean guards and gave the mercenary Krrsantan work, even though the Wookiee had tried to assassinate him.

Instead of leaving a trail of bodies, Fett created opportunities. And every time he offered an outstretched hand of mercy, it ultimately benefited him in the war against the Pykes.

EPISODE BY EPISODE

Chapter 5:
"Return of the Mandalorian"

Directed by Bryce Dallas Howard
Written by Jon Favreau
Premiered: January 26, 2022

The Mandalorian locates the survivors of his covert and fights to keep the Darksaber. Din Djarin travels to Tatooine to replace his ship and agrees to help Fennec Shand and Boba Fett.

Chapter 6:
"From the Desert Comes a Stranger"

Directed by Dave Filoni
Written by Jon Favreau and Dave Filoni
Premiered: February 2, 2022

While Din Djarin leaves Tatooine to visit Grogu, Cobb Vanth defends Freetown from spice runners. Vanth agrees to help Boba Fett until Cad Bane, working for the Pykes, threatens his town.

Chapter 7:
"In the Name of Honor"

Directed by Robert Rodriguez
Written by Jon Favreau
Premiered: February 9, 2022

War unfolds in the streets of Mos Espa as Boba Fett and his ragtag allies try to defend his territory from the Pykes and the other crime families.

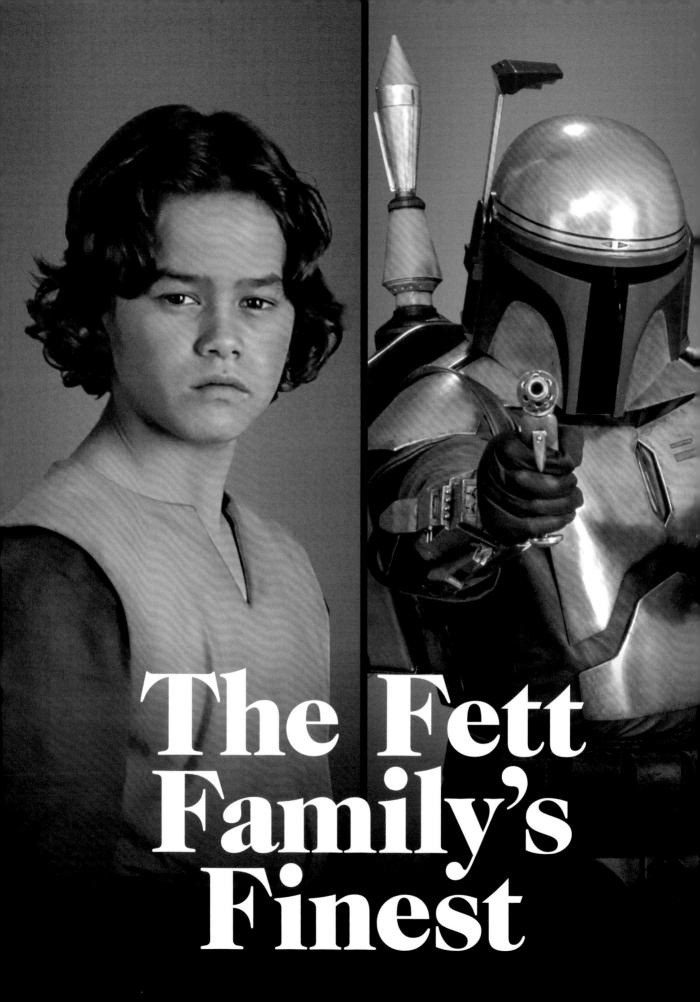

The Fett Family's Finest

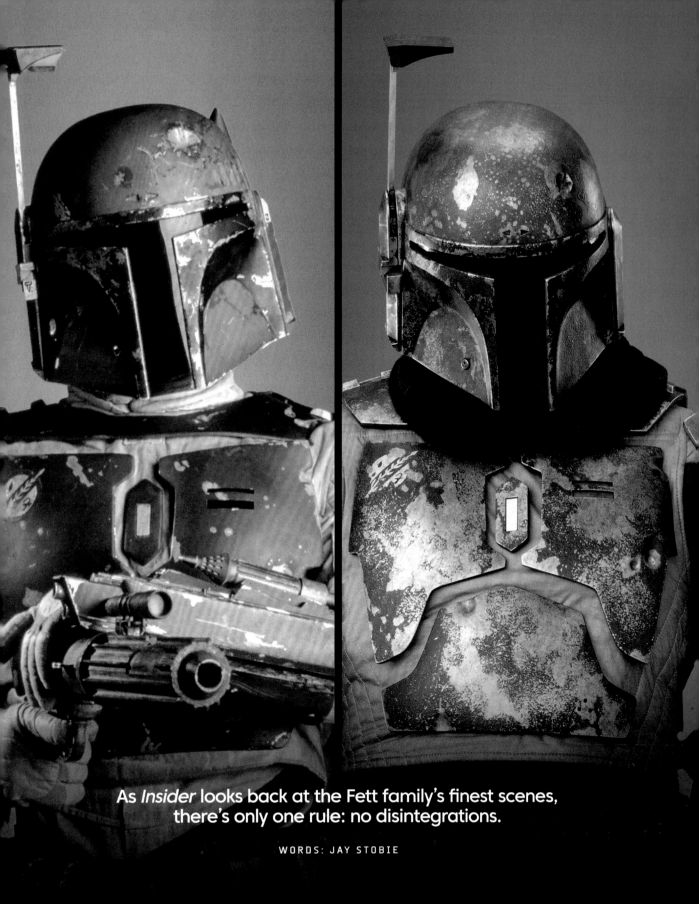

As *Insider* looks back at the Fett family's finest scenes, there's only one rule: no disintegrations.

WORDS: JAY STOBIE

10

A Special Introduction

■ The original 1978 *Star Wars Holiday Special* is infamous for many of its creative choices, but one of the attributes we can all agree on was its blisteringly entertaining introduction of bounty hunter Boba Fett.

Learning that the *Millennium Falcon* had crash-landed on a moon,

Luke Skywalker tracked down the ship, worried for the safety of his friends Han Solo and Chewbacca, only to find himself in dangerous water as he was menaced by a creature that had emerged from the inky depths. Out of nowhere an enigmatic armored figure appeared and drove the beast away, saving Luke from certain death. This was our first exciting encounter with Boba Fett, who claimed to be a friend but was actually in league with Darth Vader. With a plan to share the location of the rebel's new base with the Empire, audiences immediately recognized Fett as a bad guy—but fell in love with the cool-looking character anyway.

09

"Boba, is your father here?"

■ An innocent question from Taun We to a tousle-haired young boy on Kamino alerted audiences to the lad's true identity, as we were reintroduced to Boba Fett in *Star Wars: Attack of the Clones* (2002).

In that same scene we would quickly go on to learn that while the boy considered Jango Fett to be his father, he was actually

a genetic donor and Boba was his clone! The true magic of this breakout scene, however, came from the tense verbal stand-off between Obi-Wan Kenobi and Jango. As Kenobi attempted to subtly quiz Jango on his involvement with several assassination attempts on Senator Amidala and the origins of the clone army, the palpable friction between the pair built up in thrilling fashion, with every loaded verbal exchange as sharp as a parry between lightsabers. Jango kept his cool under the Jedi's scrutinous glare while Boba sneakily concealed the bounty hunter's Mandalorian armor from Kenobi, and the elder Fett stole the scene with his classic line: "I'm just a simple man trying to make my way in the universe."

BONUS FETT
BOBA BLASTS KENOBI

Most kids would love to drive their parents' car, but Boba Fett was living the dream when he powered up Jango's ship while his father and Kenobi fought on Kamino. Not only did he prepare the starship for its getaway and pilot it during takeoff, Boba even had the chance to fire the vessel's cannons at the pesky Jedi.

08
Messing with Mace

■ Having already fended off Kenobi on Kamino, Jango Fett was soon trading blows with another Jedi in the Geonosis arena. Jango struck the first blow with his armor's built-in flamethrower, setting Mace Windu's robes alight in the process, but the Jedi Master adeptly blocked Jango's blaster fire as he charged the bounty hunter down and decapitated him with his violet blade.

Boba bore witness to his father's death and, after the battle had moved beyond the arena, the sorrowful boy took a moment to cradle Jango's helmet lovingly to his forehead. As tragic as it was iconic, this brief mourning period signified the moment that Boba Fett inherited his father's signature armor.

07
Clone Wars Caper

■ In search of vengeance over Jango's death, Boba snuck aboard the Jedi cruiser *Endurance* so that he could plant a bomb in Mace Windu's quarters. When that failed, Boba hid among a group of clone cadets and sabotaged the vessel, causing it to crash down onto a planetary surface. Windu and Anakin Skywalker searched for survivors, only to find Jango's helmet on the bridge. Upon discovering this evidence, Windu surmised that Boba was behind the attack—just before the booby-trapped helmet nearly

killed the two Jedi! Later, Aurra Sing pressured Boba to execute Republic hostages, but the young clone hesitated and revealed a glimpse of the honor that we later saw when he assisted Din Djarin in rescuing Grogu in *The Mandalorian* (2019–present).

06

Tracking is His Trade

■ We all give Han Solo credit for the brilliant tactics he employed in escaping the Imperial fleet by disguising the *Millennium Falcon* as just another piece of junk in a Star Destroyer's ejected garbage, but we should also give Boba his due for anticipating Solo's ploy. He was also able to extrapolate the *Falcon*'s eventual destination of Bespin, thus helping Darth Vader and his stormtroopers arrive there first to spring a trap to capture the rebels.

As ingenious as the Corellian's plan was, we think Fett's own feat has gone shamelessly underappreciated. The discovery of Solo's destination set a series of events in motion that had huge repercussions for the ensuing Galactic Civil War. Imprisoning Luke Skywalker's friends lured the young Jedi to confront Vader before he was ready; freezing Solo in carbonite set the stage for a visit to Jabba the Hutt's palace; and double-crossing Lando Calrissian propelled the former smuggler into joining the Rebel Alliance's cause. As a result, young Skywalker learned Vader's true identity and felt the good in him, Jabba's criminal organization was busted wide open, and Calrissian led the assault that ultimately destroyed the second Death Star. Wait, doesn't that make Boba Fett the savior of the galaxy…?!

05

Bounty Hunter Bylaws

■ Disguised as the bounty hunter Boushh, Leia Organa brought a captive Chewbacca before Jabba the Hutt to collect the price on the Wookiee's head and gain a foothold within the palace. In typical fashion for one in Boushh's profession, Leia negotiated a higher price for her quarry than the Hutt had originally offered, with the help of a thermal detonator. After things had settled down and the Max Rebo Band were striking up another tune, Boushh and Boba Fett exchanged a knowing glance, with the latter giving a nod of approval for the former's ruthlessness. It was a subtle moment, but Boba clearly respected Boushh's desire to squeeze Jabba for as many credits as possible.

04

A Familiar Face

■ Hoping to infiltrate an Imperial facility on Morak to uncover information about Moff Gideon's whereabouts, the Mandalorian encountered a significant roadblock when he learned that the terminal storing the data required a user to remove their helmet and have their face scanned. Mando asked Boba Fett if he could complete the task, and in a rare display of dry humor, Fett alluded to his clone heritage and replied, "Let's just say they might recognize my face."

Although Fett never entered the compound, he nevertheless provided the Imperials with plenty of clues as to his true identity. In addition to flying his father's personal starship and using it as a getaway vehicle for the operation, Boba pulled a maneuver he'd picked up from his dad to destroy a squadron of TIE fighters that pursued his vessel, detonating a distinctive sounding seismic charge that wiped out the vehicles. Like father, like son.

BONUS FETT
WE KNOW THAT LOOK

Having retrieved Boba Fett's armor from Cobb Vanth, the Mandalorian and Grogu set out across the Tatooine desert to return to the *Razor Crest*, but they weren't the only ones with an interest in the battered beskar. Watching from afar, a cloaked man turned away from the sunset, his scarred face recognizable as that of a man who had evidently escaped a sarlacc pit—Boba Fett!

03

Clashing with Koska

■ More clone humor popped up when Fett and Mando attempted to enlist Bo-Katan Kryze and Koska Reeves in their quest to rescue Grogu, as Kryze recognized Fett's voice to be the same as those of the clone troopers she knew during the struggle between the Republic and the Separatists. The situation flared up, prompting Koska and Boba to engage in hand-to-hand combat—combat that also incorporated the grappling hooks, jetpacks, and flamethrowers built into their Mandalorian armor!

02

Reunited

■ Surrounded by stormtroopers from the Imperial Remnant, Mando and Fennec Shand appeared to be in quite the tough spot. Suddenly, an explosive charge fell from the sky and disoriented Moff Gideon's forces. A lone trooper heard a sound behind him, and as he turned he cast his eyes upon one of the galaxy's most frightening sites— a fully armored Boba Fett.

Fett had already dispatched quite a few stormtroopers with the Tusken gaffi stick he'd obtained on Tatooine, but being reunited with his armor turned the bounty hunter into an unstoppable, one-person army. Drawing his blaster and firing off explosive projectiles, Boba tore through Gideon's landing party with ease. As two Imperial transports attempted to flee, Fett launched a missile from his jetpack and brought down both vessels in a massive fireball. To top it off, Fett earned extra cool points by glancing at Mando and Fennec as the ships exploded behind him. Boba Fett was back.

01

Taking the Throne

■ Having served Jabba the Hutt loyally for decades, surviving the vile gangster's vicious ire on a daily basis, Bib Fortuna suddenly found himself occupying the fallen Hutt's throne one day after Jabba's sudden death. Having evidently grown accustomed to the good life over the subsequent years, he probably thought things couldn't get any better—until Fennec Shand turned up, blasted his guards, and left him defenseless. And things were about to get worse. A whole lot of Boba Fett worse.

Having ended Fortuna's career permanently in an unexpected post-credits scene at the end of *The Mandalorian*'s second season, Boba made himself comfortable on the newly vacant throne, and Fett fans rejoiced at the prospect of an entire series based on the exploits of the character we'd first met as a cartoon in 1978, or as a mail-away Kenner action figure in 1979, or in a certain classic scene from *Star Wars: The Empire Strikes Back* (1980)! However your love affair with the galaxy's greatest bounty hunter began, Fett has remained an enormously popular character from the very beginning (and he's had a few of those). With so many fine moments in the Fett family history so far, we look forward to discovering many more when the first page of *The Book of Boba Fett* opens in December 2021. 🜚

MY STAR WARS

TEMUERA MORRISON'S PERFORMANCE AS BOUNTY HUNTER JANGO FETT WAS ONE OF THE HIGHLIGHTS OF *ATTACK OF THE CLONES. INSIDER* SPOKE WITH THE NEW ZEALAND-BORN ACTOR ABOUT HIS WORK ON *STAR WARS* AND THOUGHTS ON THE SAGA AS A WHOLE. INTERVIEW: JAMES BURNS AND MARK NEWBOLD

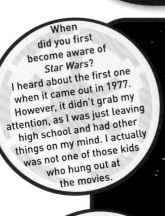

When did you first become aware of Star Wars?
I heard about the first one when it came out in 1977. However, it didn't grab my attention, as I was just leaving high school and had other things on my mind. I actually was not one of those kids who hung out at the movies.

What was your reaction to seeing Star Wars for the first time?
Like a lot of people, I thought it was quite an eye-opening experience. *Star Wars* broke through all the barriers within the industry with its special effects.

Do you have a favorite scene?
I like the scene when Darth Vader tells Luke he is his father. Wow! That was a surprise.

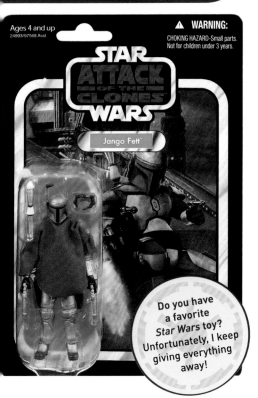
What is your favorite *Star Wars* film and why? *The Empire Strikes Back* because it had a great director... and Boba Fett.

Can you reveal something about yourself that will surprise *Star Wars* fans? I got the letter from my agent that I had a *Star Wars* meeting with Robin Gurland, the casting director. I was told that it was to take place in the Bel Age Hotel, Sunset Strip, on the 10th floor. It just so happened I was staying at the same hotel on the 9th floor. I remember looking at the letter and thinking, *Wow! A Star Wars meeting*. Robin recorded our conversation—it was simply a chat. A month or so later I received a phone call from her saying, "Tem, we would love you to play the part of Jango Fett." On hearing this news, I leapt around the room with pure delight and in the same breath said, "Who is Jango Fett?!" Of course on doing a little research I found out he is the father of Boba Fett who is a very popular character...

Where did you sign your first *Star Wars* autograph? DisneyWorld Orlando at a *Star Wars* Weekend.

Do you often get recognized? I have overheard conversations where people say, "Hey, son, that's that guy from *Once Were Warriors*, Jake the Muss." Then the son replies "No, dad, that's the guy from *Star Wars*, Jango Fett, the bounty hunter." ☻

Do you have a favorite *Star Wars* toy? Unfortunately, I keep giving everything away!

— EXPANDED —

Follow Temuera on twitter at:
@Tem_Morrison

UNIVERSE

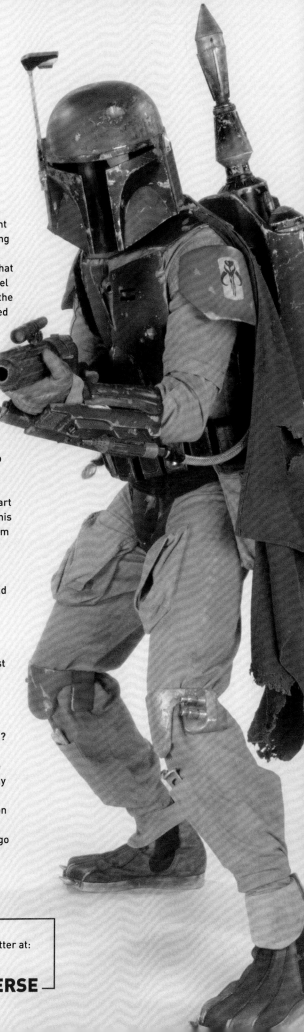

—

BOBA FETT ACTOR

DANIEL LOGAN
BOY TROUBLE

When a 13-year-old boy was called in to audition for *Star Wars*, he had no idea who the character of Boba Fett was or how playing the role was going to change his life forever. Now 31, Daniel Logan has traveled the world attending conventions, has his own collection of bounty hunter helmets and armor, and is Boba Fett's biggest fan. *Star Wars Insider* caught up with Logan to talk about his life as the galaxy's greatest bounty hunter.

WORDS: DARREN SCOTT
PHOTOS: AARON PROCTOR & MARK MEDIANA

—

What was your very first experience of the world of *Star Wars*?

When my agent called me. She was literally screaming, and said to me—out of breath, like she'd been running—that she'd gotten me an audition for *Star Wars*. I didn't have a clue what *Star Wars* was.

At that time I'd been booked for every job I was going for, so I said, "Well, send me the script and I'll get this one too." That's when she humbly replied, "No Daniel, you don't understand. This will change your life and your career. You're most likely not going to get this job, but I will forever be able to sell you as the kid who auditioned to be the kid who was in *Star Wars*."

That's when I did a little bit of research. Most people don't know that I was brought up in New Zealand, and we only had three TV channels. I was 13 years old, growing up in the period between *Star Wars: Return of the Jedi* (1983) and *Star Wars: The Phantom Menace* (1999); there had been a 16-year gap with no *Star Wars*.

Did you know what role you were going for?

I watched *The Phantom Menace*, so I figured I might be a Jedi. The casting director, Robin Gurland, asked me a bunch of questions, one of them about what I knew of *Star Wars*. Out of everyone that auditioned, I think I was probably one of the only kids who replied that I'd never really heard of or seen *Star Wars*. That might've been the thing that helped me get the part; the fact that I was a fresh, new person with no preconceptions. That I was a clean slate.

How was your audition?

I did one audition for *Star Wars*—that was it. When Robin asked me if I had any special talents, I

"I loved where we were going with *The Clone Wars*, and I was a big fan of the cartoon before I even got the opportunity to become a part of it."

told her a little white lie and said I knew, professionally, how to use the Taiaha—a traditional Māori weapon which is a stick that's been carved to use in one-on-one combat. Then she insisted that I show her how to do it, without having a stick. Obviously it was *Star Wars*, so we used our imagination and creativity. She had me imagine that I was a little Darth Maul character, and I ran around a hotel room pretending I had a double-handed lightsaber, as she moved the camera around and filmed me.

Do you think that footage still exists somewhere?

I hope so! I have no clue—I've never seen it, but I'd really like to.

When you found out you were playing Boba Fett, did you go back and watch his appearances in the original *Star Wars* movies?

You know what? I didn't until George Lucas made me. He didn't tell me that Boba Fett already had a history. I only found out about it when I went to *Star Wars* Celebration for the first time and saw the fanbase, and what kind of turnout Boba Fett had. It

03

was unbelievable. I had all these bodyguards, and people were trying to take pictures of me or touch me, just to get a glimpse of the new Boba Fett. It was incredible.

What was your first day on set like?
On my very first day I got measured for my wardrobe. That was pretty incredible. There's nothing like the smell of wardrobe; the fabric. I got fitted and also got my makeup test done, and that's when I met Ewan McGregor (Obi-Wan Kenobi) for the very first time. Although I should never have seen *Trainspotting* (1996) at my age, my big brothers had let me watch it with them, so I knew who he was. When I met him, I was totally blown away. I was reciting the *Trainspotting* lines back to him in the makeup chair, and he would trip out over the fact that I'd even seen the movie, let alone remembered his lines.

Apart from that meeting, what was the first big moment that took your breath away?
When I walked into the studio and saw the Kamino set. They'd built

entire hallways, and the Jango and Boba Fett room. Just to see the scale of it all was truly incredible. But then I got to do my first scene, which was with Temuera Morrison (Jango Fett), Ewan McGregor, and Rena Owen (Taun We). I got to act with two fellow New Zealanders in the opening scene of Boba Fett's reveal. Going through that process, Ewan actually helped me a bit with my acting, specifically to enhance the part when Obi-Wan came to visit and I opened the door. George Lucas had asked me to do a face like someone suspicious had come to the house, but as a little kid you don't have suspicion—it's not really in your toolbox of emotions. So Ewan asked me to do a face like he'd done "a very smelly fart"—they were his actual words. Growing up with a whole bunch of boys, I obviously knew that face. When I did it, he said it was perfect, but when we started rolling I opened the door, looked up to do the face, but also did a nostril flare, like I was trying to smell the fart. Ewan burst out laughing, and George started laughing his

04

01 Logan with Temuera Morrison (Jango Fett) on the set of *Attack of the Clones*.

02-04 Daniel Logan tries on a replica of Boba Fett's familiar armor.

head off. I asked, "Isn't that what you wanted?" And George replied, "Yes Daniel, everything besides the nostrils." You could see my nostrils flare up and down when he replayed the shot on the monitor. It was the funniest thing.

What was it like being a youngster on the set of such a huge film?
I was so blessed. I was on the biggest film set in the world and it was truly humbling and a honor. I'd just turned 13, and when every other ▶

LOGAN'S RUN

Born in Auckland, New Zealand in 1987, Daniel Logan was just five years old when his acting career began, after his rugby union team was scouted to appear in a TV commercial. Notching up appearances in numerous shorts and local TV shows, Logan had already amassed a number of credits by the time he won the role of the young Boba Fett in *Attack of the Clones*, for which he was nominated for a Young Artist Award for Best Performance in a Feature Film (Supporting Actor). A firm favorite on the *Star Wars* convention circuit, Logan has gone on to appear in a number of film and TV projects, including *Star Wars: The Clone Wars* TV series, in which he reprised his role as the voice of Boba. Logan now lives in California and continues to act in both film and TV.

ACTING CREDITS:

- *Underdogs Rising* (2018)
- *The Griddle House* (2018)
- *The Grindhouse Radio* (2016)
- *Sharknado 4: The 4th Awakens* (2016)
- *Star Wars: The Clone Wars* (2010-2012)
- *The Legend of Johnny Lingo* (2003)
- *TakaPu: A Gannet in the South Seas* (2003)
- *Star Wars: Attack of the Clones* (2002)
- *Falling Sparrows* (2000)
- *Hercules: The Legendary Journeys* (1999)
- *Tamatoa the Brave Warrior* (1998)
- *Shortland Street* (1992)

▶ kid was meant to be in school, I'd been given an opportunity to fly back and forth from New Zealand to Australia to do my filming gig. I'd film for a week and then I'd go home for a week or two, and then I'd go back for a couple of weeks. It was really cool, and I loved every moment because it allowed me to not only have a childhood, but to also get a glimpse of what it could be like to be respected as an adult—or a professional—in the industry.

What standout moments can you pick from that experience?
One of my other great memories was with Sir Christopher Lee (Count Dooku). I was a Nana's boy—when my mother wasn't on set, my Nana managed to come along, and I would do anything for her. One day she saw this huge, tall statue of a man standing in the dark of the studio, and she started tapping me, all excited. "Son, son, son! Oh my gosh, do you know who that is?" she said. I looked over and, you know, as a 13-year-old boy I hadn't really seen very much TV apart from cartoons. I replied, "What, some old man?" Then she informed me that the old man happened to be Sir Christopher Lee, and she was one of his biggest fans, so could I introduce her? Well, at that time I hadn't even introduced myself to Mr. Lee, but she asked so I had to do it. I took my Nana over—she was totally fan-girling out, her cheeks were red and she was blushing—and I introduced the both of us, at which point he told me how I'd been doing such a great job; he'd seen my performance as Boba and said to keep it up. I

> **"I asked Sir Christopher Lee, 'Is this your first movie?' He turned and laughed, and in a very deep, manly voice, replied, 'My boy, I have done over 150 films.'"**

replied, "Thank you very much, sir." When he asked me if it was my first film, and I replied, "Well yes, this is my first major one this year," he congratulated me. So I asked, "Is this your first movie?" He turned and laughed, and in this very deep, manly voice, replied, "My boy, I have done over 150 films." You have to remember that I was just 13 and had only done one picture a year, so in my brain I thought he was over 150 years old. I just blurted out, "Oh my gosh, you must be old!" At that point I felt like I was losing the meet-and-greet for my grandmother and needed to pull it back, so I said, "You must be 50 or 51?" With a big smile he replied and said, "My boy, you have just made my day."

What was it like working with Temuera Morrison as Jango Fett?
I loved him—and I still do, very much. When we first met he said to me, "You're going to be playing my son and I'll be playing your dad." Unfortunately, my father wasn't around when I was growing up in New Zealand, but I looked up to Tem with all of my four-foot-nothing and replied, "Okay, Dad"; he looked down at me, smiled and said, "Alright, son." Now we travel the world doing conventions

05

06

07

08

together, and we still very much have that bond.

How did you feel on your last day of filming?
That was sad—I think it might have been the scene where I was looking out over Geonosis, after Jango's head was chopped off. After I'd done the shot, George Lucas called cut and yelled for everybody to come and say goodbye. The whole production came to a stop as everyone came over and congratulated me on my job and wished me good luck. That was just such a wonderful, wonderful cast and crew. It was one of those things where you hope it will never come to an end. When it does, you have to go back to reality.

Was it strange leaving the world of Star Wars and coming back to Earth?
I went back to school, and overnight I became famous. Every person and their mom knew my name. I'd walk down the driveway of our

high school and people would say, "Hey, Daniel Logan," or "There's the Star Wars kid!" That's when I knew life would never ever be the same. You can become very, very negative towards it, but I just got very shy, and then totally embraced it. And my mom didn't have to work for nine years! [Laughs]

That wasn't your last visit to a Star Wars set though?
I did go back to the set of Star Wars: Revenge of the Sith (2005) because I was hoping to reprise the role, but unfortunately there wasn't enough story time. I had a wonderful time with George and everyone else though. They welcomed me with open arms.

What was it like doing The Clone Wars animated series?
That really brought me back to life, and it really gave the fans excitement for the character again. I loved where we were going with The Clone Wars, and I was a big fan of the cartoon

05 Daniel Logan with Ewan McGregor (Obi-Wan Kenobi).

06 Logan also played Boba Fett in six episodes of Star Wars: The Clone Wars.

07 Logan says he would return to the role of Fett "in a heartbeat."

08 The actor in full Boba Fett regalia.

"I WOULD GIVE ANYTHING TO RETURN TO THE WORLD OF STAR WARS."

before I even got the opportunity to become a part of it. It was amazing to see the vision of Lucasfilm and Dave Filoni for the world of Star Wars. I was told that George Lucas went into the storyboard room one day and said, "I want Boba Fett in The Clone Wars, call Daniel Logan." That's almost like God calling you to Heaven twice. I can't tell you how much love and respect I have for George and for everything he's done for me.

So you'd be up for a return to the Star Wars galaxy?
Oh, in a heartbeat. I would give anything to return to the world of Star Wars, and I'd love to play Boba Fett again. I train with Ray Park (Darth Maul), so I'm getting back into shape. All I see myself doing is acting. ☺

He's Worth A Lot To Me

Jeremy Bulloch: Inside Boba Fett

Boba Fett only racked up around six minutes of screen time in his first two cinematic *Star Wars* outings, but the character remains a fan favorite to this day. For Jeremy Bulloch, the first actor to play the bounty hunter on the big screen, those few minutes—or "five lines and a scream"—changed his life forever.

WORDS: DARREN SCOTT

 ounty hunter Boba Fett may have made his public debut on September 24 1978, when the character marched alongside Darth Vader in the San Anselmo Country Fair Parade, and first appeared on screen almost two months later— albeit in animated form—as part of TV *Star Wars Holiday Special*, but fans would have to wait until May 1980 to see Boba Fett on the big screen. Before securing the part, the actor charged with playing the armored mercenary was, himself, already a *Star Wars* fan.

"I did see the original *Star Wars* movie with my two young sons, and thought it something quite amazing," says Jeremy Bulloch. Little did he know that he would soon become part of one of the most celebrated film franchises of all time. "I was working in the theater in London when my half-brother, Robert Watts—the co-producer on *Star Wars: The Empire Strikes Back* (1980)—rang me and suggested I get my agent onto Lucasfilm as there was a small part of a bounty hunter that was being cast," Bulloch recalls. "I explained it would be very difficult as I was working in the theater, but he suggested that I should, 'Just give it a go.'"

Watts' gentle persuasion paid off, and Bulloch made the journey to Elstree Studios in London. "I went along and was dressed in the outfit, which fitted perfectly—even the boots were the right size—and I landed the part!"

While the outfit may have been a perfect fit, Bulloch's first encounter with the iconic armor wasn't exactly the stuff that legendary cinematic memories are made of. When faced with his Fett ensemble, he recalls with laughter that his initial reaction was, "My goodness—how do I get into that?" Donning the costume required "the help of several dressers," but the actor admits that when he finally got suited up, he was "astonished at how cool I looked." ▶

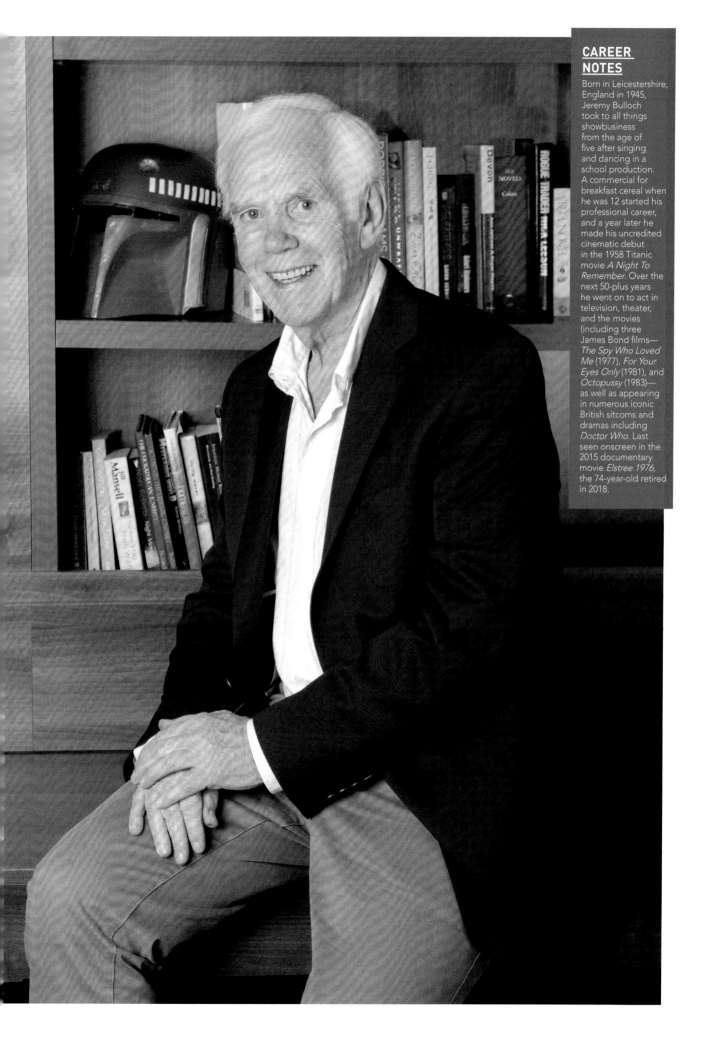

CAREER NOTES

Born in Leicestershire, England in 1945, Jeremy Bulloch took to all things showbusiness from the age of five after singing and dancing in a school production. A commercial for breakfast cereal when he was 12 started his professional career, and a year later he made his uncredited cinematic debut in the 1958 Titanic movie *A Night To Remember*. Over the next 50-plus years he went on to act in television, theater, and the movies (including three James Bond films— *The Spy Who Loved Me* (1977), *For Your Eyes Only* (1981), and *Octopussy* (1983)— as well as appearing in numerous iconic British sitcoms and dramas including *Doctor Who*. Last seen onscreen in the 2015 documentary movie *Elstree 1976*, the 74-year-old retired in 2018.

▶ With the small matter of Fett's accoutrements sorted, the time finally came for Bulloch to bring his character to life and he began filming his scenes for *The Empire Strikes Back*. "I remember the early mornings, arriving at Elstree Studios to get into the outfit, and the first time I walked onto the set as Boba Fett, everyone just stopped what they were doing to gaze at the costume," the actor recalls.

However cool the costume looked, it still presented several problems for the actor inside. "The helmet tended to steam up, which seriously affected my vision walking around the set," Bulloch says of wearing the suit in action. "And the backpack was very heavy. It became quite uncomfortable after wearing it for some time, but Boba never complained!" It was these issues with the practicality of the costume which led to one of his most famous on-screen bloopers. "I trod on Darth Vader's cape due to poor vision, and we both nearly fell on the floor. I think they edited that out," he chuckles at the memory.

The Men Behind The Mask

Despite the role being small, Bulloch wasn't the only person to play Boba

Fett during filming. "John Morton stepped in for me once because I was also appearing every night in the theater in London's West End, so therefore had to leave the studio in good time every afternoon," he explains. "That particular day they were running a bit late for the scene with Darth Vader, Boba, and Lando, so John filled in. Obviously, the stunt men stepped in for the more dangerous scenes."

Such was the popularity of the bounty hunter that he also appeared in *Star Wars: Return of the Jedi* (1983), with Bulloch happy to wear the mask once more. Fondly recalling his time on the shoot, he reveals that it was the scenes in Jabba's palace that particularly stood out for him, "because of all the extraordinary characters that were there. I was thrilled to be called back for *Return of the Jedi*, but not so thrilled to end up in the Sarlacc Pit," he laughs.

Bulloch didn't return to reprise the role in the Special Edition of *Return of the Jedi*, with Don Bies instead taking on the mantle of Boba. Re-casting—and different voices for updates—isn't something that Bulloch lets bother him, though. "It didn't worry me at all. It was Jason Wingreen who voiced the Boba Fett character in *The Empire Strikes Back* and *Return of the Jedi*, after all" he says.

With various other actors having stepped into the armor, voiced the character, or played an earlier incarnation of the notorious bounty hunter over the years, there's now an extended Boba Fett family that Bulloch is very happy to be a part of. "I get thanks from Daniel Logan for portraying the character, which indirectly led to him playing Boba as a young boy," he says of Logan's role in *Star Wars: Attack of the Clones* (2002). "Temuera Morrison, likewise, considers that his character, Jango Fett, came about because of the popularity of Boba. On the rare occasions we have gotten together at conventions, we marvel at the fact that Boba Fett played such a small role in the films but became so iconic."

> ## "The first time I walked onto the set as Boba Fett, everyone just stopped what they were doing to gaze at the costume."

01

02

03

The Public Await

Despite the huge global appeal of *Star Wars*—and the world of fandom that we know and love today—it was to be quite some time before Bulloch returned to the franchise after his initial tenure as the bounty hunter ended. "After filming, my life went back to normal; appearing in television, films, and theater productions," the actor says. "In the 1980s I was invited to two conventions—one in Florida and the other in Australia. After that, *Star Wars* was not really mentioned again until the re-release of the *Star Wars* trilogy."

Things took a different turn when a familiar, slightly foreboding, figure from the past got in touch—and as we know, when Darth Vader calls, Boba Fett doesn't say no. "Dave Prowse gave me a call and asked if I would like to go to Pasadena for a convention," Bulloch explains. "I replied that I was in the theater so it probably wouldn't be possible. I asked the producer, and surprisingly he was prepared to let me have the weekend off and put my understudy on stage, as long as I was back in time for the Monday night performance."

With his time off arranged, Bulloch packed his bag and headed off for the bright lights of Los Angeles, but nothing could have prepared him for what was in store. "When we arrived in Pasadena there were lines of people around the block to see the *Star Wars* actors!" he exclaims, even now with a modicum of disbelief. For the actor, it was the beginning of a whole new adventure in the galaxy far, far away. "It all took off from there, and the interest hasn't really ever stopped," he smiles. "I've traveled to many countries—too many to mention—and met some wonderful people. *Star Wars* fans are the same the world over."

Back In Action

This was by no means the end of his *Star Wars* journey, however, thanks to an unexpected phone call that arrived in a foreign land. "I was on holiday in Italy when my mobile

01 Bulloch also played Imperial officer Lt. Sheckil in *The Empire Strikes Back*.

02 Boba Fett's cinematic debut.

03 *Revenge of the Sith*'s Captain Colton (Jeremy Bulloch, second from left).

> ## I was thrilled to be called back for *Return of the Jedi*, but not so thrilled to end up in the Sarlacc Pit.

phone rang," Bulloch recalls. "My wife answered it and a voice said, 'Hi, it's Rick McCallum here. Can I speak to Jeremy?' We thought it was a joke, as not many people had my telephone number." Yes, that would be the same Rick McCallum who produced the prequel trilogy, the actor confirms. "He asked if I would be interested in a small part in *Star Wars: Revenge of the Sith* (2005). I was quite astonished and of course said 'Yes.' It was strange going back as a different character, but it was nice to see some old faces from the original films."

Playing Captain Colton wasn't the first time he'd appeared in *Star Wars* as someone other than Boba Fett though. "Because I was under a mask it took people quite a while to realize that I also played Lt. Sheckil in *The Empire Strikes Back*, and yes, I do get asked to sign the photo of me and Carrie Fisher," the actor fondly reveals.

Although Bulloch didn't keep any physical mementos from his time on the various *Star Wars* sets, he retained many fond memories, which in 2004 made their way into his book, *Flying Solo: Tales of a Bounty Hunter*. The book sold out and quickly became a collectors' item, and although the actor has blogged extensively on his website since the publication's release, to this day, fans are still clamoring ▶

" I'm really just an ordinary guy who got lucky wearing a very memorable suit. "

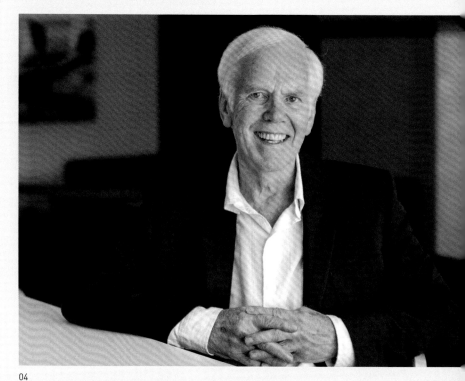

04

for a re-release or new volume. "I have thought about an update to the book," he reveals, "but it would mainly just be about conventions, which have since taken up a great part of my life." However, despite his reluctance to publish further memoirs, fans remain eager for any *Star Wars* insights the actor can share. "Over the years fans have asked many, many questions," he says with a smile. "And if I cannot answer them, I just say, 'That's classified information.'"

Bulloch is happy to offer convention advice for those newer additions to the *Star Wars* legacy. "I would suggest that they do not appear at too many conventions when they are still young, as they can take over your life," he offers with a smile. "They should carry on with their acting careers. Enjoy every moment, and be very grateful to be part of the *Star Wars* family."

04 Jeremy Bulloch.

05 Bulloch as Boba Fett in *Return of the Jedi.*

05

A Final Bounty

While Bulloch himself is still very much part of that extended family, he decided to call time on his convention appearances in 2018. "After 20 plus years of traveling around the world I thought it was time to retire, and flying is not so much fun these days," he explains.

However, while the actor may have drawn a line under his public appearances, the character he so memorably brought to life is as in demand as ever, and remains one of the most collectable when it comes to *Star Wars* merchandise. A sealed action figure of Fett made £26,040 ($34,626) in a 2016 auction, and a prototype of the rare rocket-firing version reached £18,000 ($23,933) the year before. But of all the pieces he's seen, there's one that stands out the most for the actor. "I think my favorite piece of Boba Fett merchandise is the Randy Bowen bronze statue," he says of the Dark Horse Comics release from 1997. "It's very rare and only 50 pieces were made. I'm also very fond of Boba Fett artwork, both by professional artists and fans alike."

Along with Fett merchandise, there's a whole troop of fan groups supporting the character, with forums dedicated to cosplaying as Boba hosting hundreds of thousands of messages. Bulloch fondly recalls how it was one such group that helped him stage his final appearance (to date) as the famous bounty hunter.

"The last time I put on the costume—the one that was custom made for me by members of The Dented Helmet fan troop—was July 2018, when I appeared at a big event in London," he shares. "At those shows I used to put on the outfit with the help of a couple of friends, and pose with fans for photo shoots. All the money I raised was given to Great Ormond Street Hospital, which is a brilliant children's hospital here in London. It was quite moving to know that it was probably the last time I would dress up as Boba—but you never know..."

Ever humble, the fan favorite replies with his usual grace when asked to sum up his stand-out memory from a life associated with *Star Wars*. "Being told I'm an 'icon and a legend' in my own lifetime," he says. "I'm really just an ordinary guy who got lucky wearing a very memorable suit." ☺

MY STAR WARS

JEREMY BULLOCH'S PERFORMANCE AS BOBA FETT HAS HELPED MAKE THE BOUNTY HUNTER A FAN FAVORITE—SECOND ONLY TO DARTH VADER IN *STAR WARS INSIDER*'S 2012 AWARDS. WE ASKED THE MAN BEHIND THE MASK WHAT MAKES THE SAGA SO SPECIAL TO HIM. INTERVIEW: JAMES BURNS AND MARK NEWBOLD

When did you first become aware of *Star Wars*?
When everyone seemed to be saying, "Have you seen this great sci-fi movie?"

What was your reaction to seeing *Star Wars* for the first time?
I thought I was watching something that was extraordinary. Something that would stay in the memory for a long time.

Can you reveal something about yourself that will surprise *Star Wars* fans?
I am nothing like Boba Fett. I am very gentle, especially with my 10 grandchildren. I was dangerous like Boba when I was playing soccer some years ago.

Where is the strangest place you've been recognized?
When I was waiting at a bus stop many years ago. I was in a soap opera called *The Newcomers*, and as I was getting on-board an elderly lady hit me over the head with an umbrella. In the latest episode, I had been treating my girlfriend rather badly, and she obviously took it for real!

Do you have a favorite scene?
When Darth Vader says to Boba Fett, "No disintegrations." It was my first day on the set and, despite being a calm person, I was quite nervous!

Where did you sign your first *Star Wars* autograph?
When I was in a stage play in the U.K., I was leaving the theater in Peterborough, England, after a performance of *Arms and the Man*. A fan approached me, but didn't ask about the play. He pleaded with me to sign a Boba Fett card. That was in 1983.

Do you have a favorite Star Wars toy?
A metal Boba Fett figure given to me in Japan. You wind him up and he walks!

STAR FILE
OFFICIAL BUSINESS

Boba Fett™

What is your favorite Star Wars film and why?
It has to be The Empire Strikes Back because I made my first appearance in it!

STAR WARS

The Wesell Run

By S.T. Bende

Zam Wesell lowered her macrobinoculars and dropped to her knees. The Clawdite had spent the better part of the day scouting the residence of her current target—a wealthy collector who owed a vast debt to the Intergalactic Banking Clan. Zam had known Sinvatt Bovic would go to great lengths to protect his relics— and himself. The obscured cams, regiment of security droids, and human guards patrolling his stone-walled compound would be easy to overcome. But Zam hadn't expected to find three protectors wearing purple capes with swirled, silver and black clasps. One Mabari she could handle—Zam rarely misfired, and while the ancient order of warrior-knights were nearly impervious to blaster bolts, a well-aimed shot could distract one enough to get Zam within striking range. But three working in tandem would easily overtake her. Or worse...

▶

Zam could deploy toxic gas, or set off a sizeable explosive. But both of those options carried the risk of killing Bovic. The only way to capture her target alive was to call in a favor from a formidable ally. And Zam's years with the Mabari had taught her that the only warriors Bovic's protectors truly feared wore beskar.

Zam's hands balled into fists as she crept silently back to her speeder and contacted the only bounty hunter she'd almost ever trusted.

"I need an assist," she admitted.

An emotionless voice crackled across the com. "Don't you always?"

"Do you want the credits or not?" Zam snapped. "Half the fee is yours if you help me bring in this target. And it's a big one."

After a tortuous pause, a sigh filled the cockpit. "Send me the coordinates. I'm on my way."

***

Zam's breath quickened as the familiar silhouette of Jango Fett's *Firespray*-class patrol craft touched down in the moonlit valley on Fytoun. She quickly briefed him on their assignment, checking her rifle while he checked his blasters.

"I thought you used to be Mabari." Jango crossed his arms. "What's the matter? Can't handle one of your own?"

"There are three of them." Zam said through gritted teeth. "And you're here now, so let's just get this over with and we can go our separate ways. Again."

"Whatever you say." Jango marched silently through the foliage. Zam kept a wary eye on him as they made their way to the compound and sniped the exterior cams. They decommissioned the security droids and stunned the armed humans, then inched toward the collector's inner chambers. Jango lowered his rangefinder to peer through the wall. He raised two fingers, confirming the presence of the dual Mabari stationed outside Bovic's study. The third guard must have gone out on patrol—a hurdle Zam would cross once it leaped upon her, blade drawn.

On Jango's signal, Zam detonated the wall. She ignored the sting of a shard of wooden shrapnel that grazed her cheek and charged towards the

freshly exposed hole. Jango fired two blaster bolts over her shoulder. His shots hit the Mabari, but the guards remained upright on either side of the inner chambers' imposing, crimson doors.

"Blaster bolts don't work on them!" Zam shouted, ripping her vibroblade from her belt as she raced through the gap.

"Where was that information earlier, Wesell?" Jango charged to his left. He leapt in the air and brought his elbow down on the skull of the purple-caped warrior. The Mabari barely flinched.

"Do I have to spell everything out for you?" Zam kicked a leg out in front of her, dropping low to the ground and sliding across the stones. Her heel connected with the boot of the stockier guard, and she jammed her fist into the Mabari's knee. She rolled to her left, narrowly avoiding Jango as he dodged a blow.

"You're going to get me killed." Jango grunted as his fist connected with the taller guard's chin. The Mabari spat angrily, but Zam caught the flicker of fear that passed through his eyes as he swept his gaze along Jango's Mandalorian armor.

"If that's the case, apparently I've underestimated the great Jango Fett." Zam leapt to her feet. She jabbed her vibroblade at her opponent's chest, but the guard spun and raised his own weapon—a long, curved sword that made Zam's dagger look like a Toydarian trinket. He swung it down and Zam jumped back, narrowly avoiding death by decapitation.

"That's enough," Jango muttered. "Do that thing we did on Snugano."

"I nearly died that day."

Zam dodged another swing. "Just do it. Now."

Jango raised his left arm and tapped a finger to his wrist. A projectile dart launched from his gauntlet. It whistled through the air before plunging into the wrinkled, green forehead of its victim. The guard stumbled backward, lowering his head and charging at his assailant. Jango spun swiftly. He drew a vibroblade and thrust it into the guard's thigh. The Mabari growled as he launched himself forward and slammed Jango onto the ground.

"Now, Wesell!" Jango groaned.

Zam ducked as her opponent swung his sword. A familiar ripple coursed through her as she willed her limbs to morph, and her skin to thicken. Coarse fibers burst from her flesh as she shifted into a horrifying, fur-covered beast. Hairy fingers tightened in a fist, which

> "I THOUGHT YOU USED TO BE MABARI." JANGO CROSSED HIS ARMS. "WHAT'S THE MATTER? CAN'T HANDLE ONE OF YOUR OWN?" "THERE ARE THREE OF THEM." ZAM SAID THROUGH GRITTED TEETH. "AND YOU'RE HERE NOW, SO LET'S JUST GET THIS OVER WITH."

she smashed into the startled face of her attacker. The Mabari, confused by Zam's sudden transformation, countered with a kick aimed at Zam's shin that went wide and she took fill advantage of the opening.

"Whrrraaargh!" Zam let out a feral roar, and knocked the protector into a wall. As the Mabari staggered to his feet, Zam launched a front kick that drove him to his knees. She didn't let up until her opponent lay still on the ground.

Beside her, Jango fired a series of darts at his now-limping assailant. As the Mabari clawed at the protrusions, Jango wedged a detonator beneath the clasp of the warrior's cape.

"Clear out!" he called as he flung himself across the room. Zam swiftly followed. A fierce blast rocked the hallway and she rolled to her feet, hurriedly shifting to her human form. She surveyed the bodies as Jango tilted his rangefinder toward the crimson doors, but he saw only static. "There's a scrambler blocking my scan. I guess that confirms our target is through here."

Zam wiped her face on her sleeve. "I certainly hope so."

"Are we waiting for an invitation?"

Zam glared, but swapped her blade for her blaster, squared her shoulders, and executed a swift front kick. When the doors burst open, she and Jango charged into Bovic's study. They stood back-to-back; their weapons raised as they quickly catalogued their surroundings. The circular room was lined with glass cases and multi-tiered shelves. Large, curled horns and sharply pointed fangs rested beside massive crystals and bejeweled headpieces. Tables draped with richly woven cloth displayed skulls of varying sizes, while the wall behind the smaller of the study's two desks housed the heads of a wampa, a nexu, and other creatures Zam couldn't identify.

"My bet is Bovic's up there." She pointed to the balcony, which housed an impressive display of ancient Nihil armor. The collector could have concealed himself behind one of the suits, or the arrangement of masks, or—

"Found him," Jango hissed.

The bounty hunter fired a blaster bolt which rocked the room. It bounced off the larger desk and lit up the display shelves behind it. The structure wavered—almost as if it had shifted on its foundation. A shimmering stone tumbled downward, landing at the feet of a cowering Sinvatt Bovic. The collector's navy robes fluttered as he raised trembling hands in surrender.

"Stop," he warbled. His eyes darted upward. "Please, I... you see..."

As Zam moved toward him, the third Mabari dropped lithely from the balcony. He wrapped his legs around Zam's neck, stealing her breath as he drove her to the ground. Zam tried to shoot but the warrior wrenched her blaster from her hands. As her consciousness slipped, Zam glimpsed a blur of beskar flashing in from the side. Jango slammed both his fists into the Mabari's temples, but the

a swish, a dart soared across the study. Jango fired off a blast before dropping to his knees and tearing off his helmet. Some kind of dart had penetrated his collar and was lodged firmly just beneath his jawline. He pulled the projectile from his neck, his breath coming in ragged gasps. Whatever poison the dart

▶ warrior swung one thick arm backwards, striking Jango's armor, and sending him skidding into a table. Skulls shattered on the floor as Zam grasped for her dropped vibroblade. The Mabari drove an armored knee into her wrist. Pain exploded across Zam's arm, and she bit down on the inside of her cheek. Her captor arced his silver sword in what would surely be a killing blow. But before he could strike, a sharp hiss pierced the air. Jango's grappling hook wrapped around the Mabari's neck and lodged into his cape-clad shoulder. The guard roared as he was wrenched away from his prize. He landed with a resounding crack, his body crumpling below the wall of mounted heads.

Zam pushed herself up with a shaky, "Thanks."

"You always did need me to save you."

A low growl built in Zam's throat while she retrieved her blaster. "I'll have you know, I—"

Crash!

Zam turned her head just as Bovic shoved one robed arm into the nearest display. He withdrew an elongated blowgun and raised it to his lips. With

contained, it had already entered his bloodstream.

A clatter behind her let Zam know that Bovic was down. She turned to find the collector shuddering violently. His eyes rolled back in his head as he crumpled to the ground, landing on his back on the stones. When his body went limp, Zam swore.

"You killed our target! You blew this job—just like last time! I told you this was no dead-or-alive assignment, Fett. We needed him—"

A coat of green morphed quickly across Bovic's skin as his human form yielded into a surprisingly familiar shape. The man's cheekbones protruded sharply and his forehead took on a reptilian sheen. Zam gasped. This wasn't Bovic at all, but another Clawdite—something she'd not accounted for while reconning the building. But how had the real Bovic escaped? And where was he now?

Her eyes darted to the display shelf. Could it possibly be a—?

"Zam!" Jango's cry pulled her back. The bounty hunter was crawling across the sea of shattered artifacts, his breathing giving way to fluid-filled coughs.

Zam's gaze shifted between her partner and the shelf. Jango had been poisoned, but their target was getting away, and every second that passed diminished her odds of completing this job. As Jango convulsed into a desperate coughing fit, Zam made up her mind. She turned on her heel and raced across the study. She leapt over the stunned Clawdite, swiftly sized up the display, and tore the priceless objects from its shelves. Surely, an activator was built in somewhere! But the items crashed uselessly to the ground—none triggered whatever catch might open a secret passageway.

"Hey!" Jango choked.

Zam quickly scanned the room. If she couldn't open the wall, she'd blow it off its foundation. But Bovic's collection was sorely lacking in detonators, and she'd already used up her own supply. Maybe if the study housed a vibro-ax, or if one of the suits of Nihil armor contained something explosive. There had to be something in here she could use...

"Za-am!" Jango rasped her name. The bounty hunter reluctantly shifted her focus towards her ailing partner. Then her gaze landed on the projectile

know that rancid stench anywhere. We have to locate an antivenin."

Jango pointed to the shattered case. "Try the cabinet that held—cough—the blowgun—cough—"

"I see it." Zam hurdled over the toppled form of a well-preserved eopie. A simple clay jar sat at the rear of the cabinet, unbroken. She pulled open its cap and peered at its shimmering, yellow contents before returning to Jango. "It looks like what I remember of antivenin, but if we're wrong this isn't going to end well."

Jango snatched the jar from her hands. "That's a risk I'm willing to take." With a wry nod, he downed the liquid in two loud gulps.

Zam shifted from one foot to the other. "You good?"

"Give it a minute." He wheezed. "How about now?"

Jango pushed himself to his feet.

a cramped hangar, where a red speeder sat beneath an oval window. Moonlight streamed through the transparisteel, illuminating the real Bovic as he struggled to open the sealed cockpit.

"Oh, no you don't," Zam hissed. She lined up her shot and sniped the ship's airlock controls. Before Bovic could turn around, she flipped a switch and fired off a second shot—one that stunned her target into submission.

"You positive that's not another changeling?" Jango called as he walked across the silent hangar.

Zam poked a gloved finger into Bovic's cheek. The doughy, white flesh bore no hints of green. "I hope not."

"Then let's get him bound and delivered to the client. Believe it or not, I do have my own targets to acquire."

"I can take him from here." Zam pulled a set of binders from her belt and fastened them to Bovic's wrists. She and Jango maneuvered the sizeable man out of the now-silent compound and loaded him into Zam's speeder.

Once their prize was secure, Jango offered a curt salute. "You know where to send my credits."

Zam tilted her head. "You may want to lower your percentage, given the fact that I saved your life."

"Maybe I would, if I hadn't done the same for you."

The bounty hunters traded begrudging nods. Zam kept one hand on the hilt of her blaster as Jango walked swiftly toward his blue-and-silver Firespray. She had no doubt that their paths would cross again. They always did. Every so often it helped to have a partner... even one she might never fully trust.

THE END

ZAM STEPPED BACK AS THE ROCKET LAUNCHED. IT SLAMMED INTO THE WOOD, IGNITING A SPRAY OF SPLINTERED SHARDS AS THE WALL ERUPTED IN A BLAZE OF FIERY GLORY.

in Jango's jetpack, and a wave of relief washed through her.

"Fire your rocket at the display shelf," she demanded. "It disguises the entrance to a passage—one that just gave Bovic the perfect escape route."

Jango clawed at his chest. "Help me first."

"I don't have time," Zam snapped.

"Do it. Or I'll fire this rocket at you."

Zam narrowed her eyes. "You wouldn't," she growled.

"I have nothing to lose, and you know it."

Zam quickly weighed her options. With a frustrated groan, she sprinted across the study. She knelt at Jango's side, picked up the dart, and slid it beneath her nose. The sharp tang of venom sent a shudder along her spine. "Bluebarb wasp," she spat. "I'd

"Your bedside manner never was your strong suit."

Zam crossed her arms. "I'll take that as a yes. Now blast through that wall."

Jango lowered his shoulders and angled his spine toward the shelves. Zam stepped back as the rocket launched. It slammed into the wood, igniting a spray of splintered shards as the wall erupted in a blaze of fiery glory. A surge of heat rumbled through the study, and Zam flung her arms up to shield her face against the burn. The moment the fire ebbed, Zam charged through the still-smoking passage.

"You planning to join me?" she shouted over her shoulder.

The pad of Jango's footfalls echoed behind her as she raced toward the faint shaft of light streaming from the end of the tunnel. She emerged inside

STAR WARS LIBRARY

STAR WARS: THE MANDALORIAN GUIDE TO SEASON ONE

STAR WARS: THE MANDALORIAN GUIDE TO SEASON TWO

STAR WARS: THE EMPIRE STRIKES BACK: THE 40TH ANNIVERSARY SPECIAL EDITION

STAR WARS INSIDER: THE FICTION COLLECTION VOLUME 2

STAR WARS: THE SKYWALKER SAGA THE OFFICIAL COLLECTOR'S EDITION

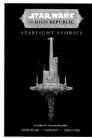
STAR WARS: THE HIGH REPUBLIC: STARLIGHT STORIES VOLUME 1

- *ROGUE ONE: A STAR WARS STORY* THE OFFICIAL COLLECTOR'S EDITION
- *ROGUE ONE: A STAR WARS STORY* THE OFFICIAL MISSION DEBRIEF
- *STAR WARS: THE LAST JEDI* THE OFFICIAL COLLECTOR'S EDITION
- *STAR WARS: THE LAST JEDI* THE OFFICIAL MOVIE COMPANION
- *STAR WARS: THE LAST JEDI* THE ULTIMATE GUIDE
- *SOLO: A STAR WARS STORY* THE OFFICIAL COLLECTOR'S EDITION
- *SOLO: A STAR WARS STORY* THE ULTIMATE GUIDE
- THE BEST OF *STAR WARS INSIDER* VOLUME 1
- THE BEST OF *STAR WARS INSIDER* VOLUME 2

- THE BEST OF *STAR WARS INSIDER* VOLUME 3
- THE BEST OF *STAR WARS INSIDER* VOLUME 4
- *STAR WARS:* LORDS OF THE SITH
- *STAR WARS:* HEROES OF THE FORCE
- *STAR WARS:* ICONS OF THE GALAXY
- *STAR WARS:* THE SAGA BEGINS
- *STAR WARS* THE ORIGINAL TRILOGY
- *STAR WARS:* ROGUES, SCOUNDRELS AND BOUNTY HUNTERS
- *STAR WARS:* CREATURES, ALIENS, AND DROIDS
- *STAR WARS: THE RISE OF SKYWALKER* THE OFFICIAL COLLECTOR'S EDITION
- *STAR WARS: THE MANDALORIAN*: GUIDE TO SEASON ONE
- *STAR WARS: THE MANDALORIAN*: GUIDE TO SEASON TWO

- *STAR WARS: THE EMPIRE STRIKES BACK* THE 40TH ANNIVERSARY SPECIAL EDITION
- *STAR WARS: AGE OF RESISTANCE* THE OFFICIAL COLLECTORS' EDITION
- *STAR WARS: THE SKYWALKER SAGA* THE OFFICIAL COLLECTOR'S EDITION
- *STAR WARS INSIDER: FICTION COLLECTION* VOLUME 1
- *STAR WARS INSIDER PRESENTS: MANDALORIAN SEASON 2* VOLUME 1
- *STAR WARS INSIDER PRESENTS: MANDALORIAN SEASON 2* VOLUME 2
- *STAR WARS: THE HIGH REPUBLIC: STARLIGHT STORIES* VOLUME 1

MARVEL STUDIOS LIBRARY

MOVIE SPECIALS
- MARVEL STUDIOS' *SPIDER-MAN: FAR FROM HOME*
- MARVEL STUDIOS' *ANT-MAN AND THE WASP*
- MARVEL STUDIOS' *AVENGERS: ENDGAME*
- MARVEL STUDIOS' *AVENGERS: INFINITY WAR*
- MARVEL STUDIOS' *BLACK PANTHER* (COMPANION)
- MARVEL STUDIOS' *BLACK WIDOW*
- MARVEL STUDIOS' *CAPTAIN MARVEL*
- MARVEL STUDIOS: THE FIRST TEN YEARS
- MARVEL STUDIOS' *THOR: RAGNAROK*
- MARVEL STUDIOS' *AVENGERS: AN INSIDER'S GUIDE TO THE AVENGERS' FILMS*
- MARVEL STUDIOS' *THE FALCON AND THE WINTER SOLDIER*
- MARVEL STUDIOS' *WANDAVISION*

MARVEL STUDIOS' LOKI: THE OFFICIAL MARVEL STUDIOS COLLECTOR SPECIAL

MARVEL STUDIOS' ETERNALS: THE OFFICIAL MOVIE SPECIAL

MARVEL STUDIOS' SPIDER-MAN: NO WAY HOME: THE OFFICIAL MOVIE SPECIAL

MARVEL STUDIOS' DOCTOR STRANGE IN THE MULTIVERSE OF MADNESS: THE OFFICIAL MOVIE SPECIAL

MARVEL LEGACY LIBRARY

MARVEL'S CAPTAIN AMERICA: THE FIRST 80 YEARS

MARVEL: THE FIRST 80 YEARS

MARVEL'S DEADPOOL: THE FIRST 30 YEARS

MARVEL'S FANTASTIC FOUR: THE FIRST 60 YEARS

MARVEL'S SPIDER-MAN: THE FIRST 60 YEARS

MARVEL'S HULK: THE FIRST 60 YEARS

MARVEL CLASSIC NOVELS
- WOLVERINE WEAPON X OMNIBUS
- SPIDER-MAN THE DARKEST HOURS OMNIBUS
- SPIDER-MAN THE VENOM FACTOR OMNIBUS
- X-MEN AND THE AVENGERS GAMMA QUEST OMNIBUS
- X-MEN MUTANT EMPIRE OMNIBUS

NOVELS
- MARVEL'S GUARDIANS OF THE GALAXY NO GUTS, NO GLORY
- SPIDER-MAN MILES MORALES WINGS OF FURY
- MORBIUS THE LIVING VAMPIRE: BLOOD TIES
- ANT-MAN NATURAL ENEMY
- AVENGERS EVERYBODY WANTS TO RULE THE WORLD

- AVENGERS INFINITY
- BLACK PANTHER WHO IS THE BLACK PANTHER?
- CAPTAIN AMERICA DARK DESIGNS
- CAPTAIN MARVEL LIBERATION RUN
- CIVIL WAR
- DEADPOOL PAWS
- SPIDER-MAN FOREVER YOUNG
- SPIDER-MAN KRAVEN'S LAST HUNT
- THANOS DEATH SENTENCE
- VENOM LETHAL PROTECTOR
- X-MEN DAYS OF FUTURE PAST
- X-MEN THE DARK PHOENIX SAGA
- SPIDER-MAN HOSTILE TAKEOVER

ART BOOKS
- *THE GUARDIANS OF THE GALAXY* THE ART OF THE GAME
- MARVEL'S *AVENGERS: BLACK PANTHER: WAR FOR WAKANDA* THE ART OF THE EXPANSION
- MARVEL'S *SPIDER-MAN MILES MORALES* THE ART OF THE GAME
- MARVEL'S *AVENGERS* THE ART OF THE GAME
- MARVEL'S *SPIDER-MAN* THE ART OF THE GAME
- MARVEL *CONTEST OF CHAMPIONS* THE ART OF THE BATTLEREALM
- *SPIDER-MAN: INTO THE SPIDER-VERSE* THE ART OF THE MOVIE
- THE ART OF IRON MAN THE ART OF THE MOVIE